DRAGONS

Jonathan Evans

VICTOR CARPATHIVS VENETVS·O·

DRAGONS

a beautifully illustrated quest for the world's great dragon myths

Jonathan Evans

METRO BOOKS
NEW YORK

INTRODUCTION

Dragons and dragon myths are ubiquitous in world history and culture. From ancient Babylonian creation stories to Icelandic sagas, from Chinese art and legend to Renaissance epic poetry, we find monstrous serpents—often winged, sometimes breathing fire—inspiring awe, terror, and admiration. The dragon has been described in many different ways, with many different kinds of mythic significance, in world mythology. Is the dragon a friend or an enemy? Is it primarily protective or destructive? What does the dragon myth mean? What, in fact, does a dragon look like? In order to answer these questions, the origins and development of the dragon myth must be untangled.

Eastern dragons
DESPITE THEIR FEARFUL APPEARANCE, WITH BULGING EYES, HUGE JAWS, AND FIERCE TEETH, EASTERN DRAGONS TEND TO BE BENEVOLENT IN NATURE, BRINGING GOOD FORTUNE AND WEALTH.

Chinese dragon shadow puppet
THE DRAGON HAS BEEN AN EMBLEM OF THE
CHINESE IMPERIAL FAMILY SINCE ANCIENT
TIMES. IN CHINESE YIN-YANG COSMOLOGY,
THE DRAGON REPRESENTED YANG, THE
PRINCIPAL OF MALENESS.

ORIGINS OF THE DRAGON MYTH

There are two theories as to how the dragon myth began. According to the first theory, the story originated in a specific part of the world, spreading and developing over a long period of time into the myths now associated with the ancient cultures of Egypt, Mesopotamia, India, and China. C. G. Child's *The Natural History of Dragons* traces the monster's origins to a host of serpents, water-creatures, and other reptiles in the ancient Near East. The Western dragon myth, he says, is a development from the Babylonian creation myth of Marduk's slaying of Ti'amat, the serpent-monster, or of Indra's slaying of Vritra in the Hindu myth. One or other of these stories developed into the Greek myth and Christian religion, thus entering the mainstream of Western literature.

Since some of the oldest dragon myths come from Mesopotamia, Joseph Fontenrose suggests that the myth originated there, spreading westward into Greece and from there across the Mediterranean world into Europe, while in its eastward migrations it entered India and inspired Hindu versions of the story. Fontenrose also speculates that the myth could have traveled further east into China: the Nagas, evil snake-demons of the underworld, he says, were "imported with Buddhism from India," and are distinctly different from the generally benevolent native dragons of pre-Buddhist China.

UNIVERSAL FEAR

The second theory of dragon origins supposes the myth took shape independently in many different places, expressing a universal fear of poisonous serpents, snakes, and reptiles. As ancient cultures spread, these independent myths began to overlap and influence one another, generating the classic concept of the dragon in medieval and Renaissance Europe. This would explain the dragon-like monsters in myths of the western hemisphere that have no connection to Asian or European influence—for example, the quetzalcoatl (meaning "bird-serpent") of Meso-American mythology, and the amhuluk, palulukon, angont, and kolowisi in Hopi, Huron, and Zuni religions.

This theory is supported by the many different physical forms the dragon has been given over the last four millennia: some early descriptions and visual representations suggest it was composed from the body parts of many different animals. Even the Chinese dragon did not have a definite description. In *Chinese Dragons*, Roy Bates says:

"THE CHINESE ... HAD PALPABLE BEASTS LIKE SNAKES,
ALLIGATORS, HORSES, AND TIGERS
THAT COULD BE SEEN AND STUDIED,
AND THEIR SHAPE COULD BE COPIED.
YET THE DRAGON WAS ALWAYS INTANGIBLE.
ITS SHAPE, AND ITS CHARACTERISTICS,
VARIED FROM PLACE TO PLACE."

Gold dragon

A VARIETY OF ANIMALS COULD HAVE INSPIRED DRAGON MYTHS; THE DRAGON ABOVE LOOKS SOMEWHAT SNAKELIKE, WHILE OTHERS SHARE PHYSICAL FEATURES WITH CROCODILES, BIRDS, OR DINOSAURS.

DRAGONS, EAST AND WEST

Chinese altar cover

(RIGHT) THIS CHINESE ALTAR COVER WITH A DRAGON MOTIF DATES TO AROUND 1600. DESIGNS FEATURING DRAGONS WERE COMMONLY USED IN CHINESE TEXTILES AND ON CARPETS.

In the Chinese version of the dragon myth, the dragon appears as a protective force associated with the life-giving natural world, particularly water. By contrast, Western traditions emphasize the destructive implications of its power, and in Classical and medieval European mythologies, dragons appear as cosmic enemies of heroic warriors and saintly defenders against evil. Both these traditions may originate in Near Eastern creation myths that represent unformed chaos as a monstrous dragon in mortal combat against the divine, life-giving forces of order and creation. Asian dragon myths are without a doubt the most interesting visually, providing the world with some of the most beautiful painting, sculpture, enamel work, and architectural representations of the monster, while the myths, legends, and folktales of the Western tradition generally make more interesting stories.

Rooftop dragons

(BELOW) TWO ROOFTOP DRAGONS ADORN THIS 18TH-CENTURY CHINESE SHRINE IN BANGKOK, THAILAND. BUILT BY CHINESE MIGRANTS TO THAILAND, THE DRAGONS ARE A POTENT SYMBOL OF CHINESE CULTURE.

THE DRAGON AS MYTH

This book treats the dragon not as a fictional figure in literature or folklore but as a myth. For anthropologists, historians, and students of religion and mythology, myths record what people believe about the world: how the universe was made, where human beings came from, how we fit into the scheme of nature, and how the world might end. Whether these stories have any basis in historical fact or can be proven to be objectively true does not matter. What matters is that people used them to make sense of the world around them. "What does the dragon myth mean?" isn't the same as asking, "Is the dragon myth true?" The first question depends upon the second and assumes the second answer is "Yes."

MODERN DRAGON LORE

While it is an ancient figure, the dragon is found so often in popular culture that in some respects it can still be regarded as a living myth. A survey of modern survivals of the dragon myth might begin with Ernest Drake's *Dragonology* books, for example, and the games and modeling kits based upon them. We should include fantasy novels by writers such as Jane Yolen and Orson Scott Card; Anne McCaffrey's *Dragonriders* series; and the *Dragonlance* books by many authors. There are also innumerable web sites devoted to dragons, dragon lore, and dragon mythology.

Most conceptions of the dragon in modern fairy tales, fantasy literature, internet subcultures, and juvenile fiction are not recent inventions—they originated in the myths of ancient cultures. But as an ongoing creative source of art and storytelling, over the last four millennia the dragon has survived many transformations. For many, the dragon is still alive.

Angelica held captive by a dragon
THIS 1873 PAINTING BY ARNOLD BOCKLIN ILLUSTRATES A COMMON THEME IN WESTERN DRAGON STORIES: A PRINCESS IS SAVED FROM A DRAGON'S CLUTCHES BY A VIRTUOUS HERO. THE HERO WILL SLAY THE DRAGON AND MARRY THE PRINCESS.

THE MEANING OF THE DRAGON

Regardless of its origins and the variety of meanings it has acquired in later history, it is clear that the dragon myth combines different elements of diverse origin; it has multiple meanings, and cannot be reduced to a single interpretive message. The dragon myths summarized in this book fall into four main traditions; four main categories of meaning. Though a precise chronology cannot be determined, these four traditions may be arranged as follows:

✤ *Ancient Near East.* In creation myths of ancient Egypt, India, and Mesopotamia, the dragon represents the destructive waters of chaos and death, the enemy of the gods of creation, life, and order. The mythic slaying of this dragon is an essential cosmic event enabling the creation of the world. The dragon embodies cosmic evil, and the story of its defeat by the divine hero is a positive mythic event. Elements of this tradition survive in biblical material and later influenced the European dragon tradition.

✤ *Asia.* The dragon in this part of the world is also associated with water—clouds, rain, rivers, lakes, and oceans—as a creative or protective force. The Chinese Dragon Kings represent divine protective power, opposed to the forces of evil and ultimately benevolent to human interests. The pictorial tradition perpetuates this essential symbolism and influences how Westerners typically imagine the dragon's appearance.

❧ **Ancient Greece.** In ancient Greece the dragon embodies cosmic evil, opposed to divine forces. Later influenced by biblical traditions rooted in Mesopotamian mythology, this idea spread into Europe, where it combined with local myths reflecting the perspectives of their respective cultures. Thor's fight with the Midgard Serpent is a Germanic version; in Beowulf and the Sigurd legend, dragons symbolize the destructive effects of excessive wealth and power.

❧ **European/Biblical.** In the biblical myth, the dragon represents Satan, the fallen angel of Hebrew and Christian scriptures. This version generated many stories of saints' battles with dragons, the best-known being the St. George legend.

Modern versions of the dragon myth borrow from these four traditions, often combining them. However, these versions usually just make reference to the earlier traditions—they are not active expressions of mythic truth.

DRAGONS TODAY

Earlier, we said that the dragon myth, in some respects, is still alive. So we must add a fifth category; a fifth tradition. Jay Williams's children's book, *Everyone Knows What A Dragon Looks Like,* tells the story of the Chinese city of Wu which is threatened by invading horsemen:

> THE CITY'S RULER COMMANDS THE PEOPLE TO PRAY FOR THE HELP OF THE CLOUD DRAGON, AND THE NEXT DAY A LITTLE FAT MAN APPEARS AT THE CITY GATES CLAIMING TO BE A DRAGON COME TO RESCUE THEM, IF THEY WILL INVITE HIM IN AND FEED HIM. THE PEOPLE SCOFF, SINCE THEY ALL KNOW WHAT A DRAGON LOOKS LIKE, AND IT DOESN'T LOOK LIKE HIM. ONLY ONE LITTLE ORPHAN WILL INVITE THE OLD MAN INTO THE CITY AND OFFER HIM FOOD. BECAUSE OF THE LITTLE BOY'S KINDNESS, THE OLD MAN AGREES TO DEFEND THE CITY, WHEREUPON HE CHANGES INTO THE FAMILIAR CHINESE DRAGON WITH SCALES AND CLAWS AND TEETH, AND DEFEATS THE INVADERS.

Neither the Mandarin nor any of his councilors knows what a dragon looks like nor where its power really comes from. The dragon reveals its true appearance only to a child—and, significantly, to the reader. In Williams's book the ability to see what others cannot is given to a child whose imagination has not been clouded by sophisticated civilization. The fifth dragon myth, then, may be described as follows:

❧ **Modern.** The dragon is a symbol of the wonder of the world which Tolkien described as "the perilous realm of faërie": fairy tales, fantasy literature, and imaginative fiction. Dragons in modern popular culture have mythic meaning on two levels: first, as historicized allusions to earlier dragon myths; second, as symbolic references to the idea of dragons, thriving in that most fertile, fascinating, and endlessly creative realm of all: the human imagination.

The Jabberwock

THIS UNDATED ILLUSTRATION FROM LEWIS
CARROLL'S *THROUGH THE LOOKING
GLASS* ACCOMPANIES HIS NONSENSE POEM
JABBERWOCKY. THE POEM DESCRIBES THE
JABBERWOCK'S DRAGONLIKE FEATURES: "THE
JAWS THAT BITE, THE CLAWS THAT CATCH!"

eastern DRAGONS

Chinese dragon, Singapore
THIS SEMI-RELIEF OF A SERPENTLIKE DRAGON
COMES FORM HAW PAR VILLA IN SINGAPORE;
IT WAS BUILT IN 1937.

eastern dragon mythology

Confucius Temple, Qufu

A DETAIL OF THE DRAGON RELIEF ON ONE
OF THE TEN COLUMNS IN THE TEMPLE IN
QUFU, THE BIRTHPLACE OT THE CHINESE
PHILOSOPHER CONIFICUS (551–479 BCE).
THESE EXQUISITELY CARVED DRAGONS ARE
EXTREMELY RARE.

The dragon myths of the ancient Near East and Asia are the oldest in the world. In Mesopotamia, the cycle of narratives that includes Baal's defeat of Yamm was composed about 1375 BCE, and based on material from the third millennium BCE. This mythic tradition also contributed to the religious traditions evident in the Bible, where Yahweh—whose enemy is the rival deity Baal—is also described as the vanquisher of Leviathan (Job 41, Psalm 74, and Isaiah 27). Though the Marduk and Ti'amat myth was discovered in cuneiform texts dating from the time of Ahurbanipal (668–630 BCE), the story itself was probably composed about 1100 BCE from material from early in the second millennium, and it also has affinities with biblical traditions.

The Rig Veda, which contains many hymns celebrating Indra's victory over Vritra, reached its present form in about 1000 BCE but exemplifies a mythic tradition that originated around 2000 BCE and perhaps earlier.

Egypt's religious rituals connected with the sun god Ra, the storm god Set, and the dragon of the underworld Apep, originated at about the same time as the development of hieroglyphics and the establishment of Memphis, *circa* 3000 BCE.

In the Far East, the conceptions of the dragon as a weather god or as a divine protector of water originated as early as the Hongshan culture in China, from about 3500 to 2000 BCE. The dragon is mentioned in the Yijing or I-Ching, *The Book of Changes*, from the Zhou dynasty, around 1027–221 BCE, and dragon figures have been unearthed from about 4000 BCE in the Yellow and Liao river basins.

DRAGONS AS SYMBOLS

The precise relationship between these and other dragon myths from the earliest civilizations we know about cannot be established with precision. But the similarities between them stand out clearly: in many of the earliest myths, the dragon is a force associated with bodies of water and symbolic of darkness, disorder, and death. A god fights and defeats the dragon, eliminating a source of chaos and sometimes releasing benevolent water for the benefit of mankind.

Chinese dragon mythology seems to stand apart from the Near-Eastern tradition which, with its dragon-slaying divine hero, seems closer to Greek myths and later European ones. Asian dragons tend to symbolize positive values cherished by indigenous Chinese, Japanese, Korean, and related cultures. In mythic terms, Asian dragons typically do not perform the crucial narrative role of antagonist against divine, semi-divine, or

Dragon gods

IN THIS 20TH-CENTURY ILLUSTRATION FROM *MYTHS AND LEGENDS OF CHINA* BY E.T.C. WERNER, DRAGONS AND THEIR RIDERS FLY THROUGH THE CLOUDS. ACCORDING TO CHINESE MYTHOLOGY, DRAGONS COULD CREATE CLOUDS WITH THEIR BREATH.

Gilded Chinese dragon

THIS ENGRAVED AND GILDED JADE DRAGON APPEARS ON THE COVER OF *THE SONG OF THE JADE BOWL*, WRITTEN BY THE CHINESE EMPEROR QIANLONG IN 1745.

human heroic combatants. Instead, they symbolize divine benevolence or protective imperial power, associated with the life-giving force of water in its various natural forms: rain, rivers, lakes, and oceans.

However, in the Shu Ching, an early Chinese creation myth, the high God sends his emissaries to clear the earth, which is covered with water, for human habitation. They are resisted by dragons and horned water-monsters until God sends Yü, who defeats the dragons, banishing the chief monster to an island. In a later version, the Yellow Emperor sends a winged dragon called Ying Lung to defeat a river monster called Ch'ih Yu. Ying Lung gathers the waters of the earth against the monster, who uses wind and rain as his weapons, and in the ensuing battle the world is flooded.

Another Chinese myth, the story of the divine archer Shên Yi, similarly begins with a water-covered earth. Wind storms wrought destruction everywhere, the sun was ten times its normal heat, and a thousand-foot-long serpent caught men and animals, and ate them beside Tung-T'ing Lake. Emperor Yao sent the archer Yi, who killed the serpent and the lord of winds, an old man in the form of a winged dragon.

THE STORY OF STORIES

Joseph Fontenrose sees similarities between these Chinese mythic patterns and the underlying patterns of the Mesopotamian and early Greek myths examined later in this book. Fontenrose says that while the Chinese dragon myth may be a "spontaneous growth," the similarities are nothing short of "remarkable," and further speculates that the dragon myth could have "traveled quite early from Mesopotamia or India to China."

By and large, however, in the myths of later Imperial China, the pattern of cosmic combat identified in these early sources has been replaced by a dragon mythology in which dragons remain powerful but benign. The arrival of Buddhism in China late in the last century BCE or early in the first century CE led to a reorganization of China's mythic system, and China's dragons usually came to represent positive, not negative, natural forces.

If the dragon fight is the story underlying Western mythology—the "story of stories," so to speak—the dragon myths of the Asian world seem to have been preserved largely in non-narrative modes; such stories often come from more recent, not ancient, sources. China and Japan, however, have produced some of the most beautiful artistic representations of the dragon, which began to influence Western pictorial traditions in the 18th and 19th centuries. Just as China may have received some of its dragon mythology through prehistoric contacts with Near Eastern or Mediterranean myths, modern conceptions of the monster—even those strictly within the Western tradition of mythic enemies fighting divine heroes—have been influenced by Asian art.

Jade dragon pendant
HIS PENDANT IN THE SHAPE OF A DRAGON, INSPIRED BY AN ANCIENT CHINESE DESIGN, DATES TO THE 18TH OR 19TH CENTURY. DRAGON MOTIFS APPEARED ON JADE ARTIFACTS IN CHINA AS FAR BACK AS THE HONGSHAN PERIOD (C. 3500–2200 BCE).

> **" THE CHINESE DRAGONS CAN BE DIVIDED INTO TWO CLASSES: THE NATIVE CHINESE (I.E., PRE-BUDDHISTIC) DRAGONS AND THE NAGAS, IMPORTED WITH BUDDHISM FROM INDIA. THE CHINESE DRAGONS ARE IN GENERAL BENEVOLENT AND BENEFICENT DEITIES, WHO SEND RAIN AND BRING GOOD CROPS... LIKE ZEUS OR BAAL, THEY BRING BOTH GOOD AND BAD WEATHER; FOR THE GOD, WE SHOULD NOT FORGET, CAN SEND BOTH GOOD AND EVIL UPON MORTAL MEN. "**
> JOSEPH FONTENROSE, 1974, *PYTHON: A STUDY OF DELPHIC MYTH AND ITS ORIGINS*

Two dragons in clouds

A 19TH-CENTURY PAINTING BY JAPANESE
ARTIST KANO HOGAI. ACCORDING TO
JAPANESE AND CHINESE FOLKLORE, DRAGONS
ARE ASSOCIATED WITH RAIN, STORMS,
AND CLOUDS, AND ARE RESPONSIBLE FOR
PRODUCING RAIN.

Urashima and the Dragon Kings

DRAGONS IN JAPAN ARE ASSOCIATED WITH WATER, JUST AS THEY ARE IN CHINESE DRAGON MYTHS, AND JAPAN HAS ITS OWN RICH MYTHIC TRADITIONS OF DRAGON KINGS WHO LIVE IN THE SEA. *THE NIHONGI*, OR "CHRONICLES OF JAPAN," WHICH WAS COMPILED IN THE 8TH CENTURY, TELLS OF HOW THE SKY GOD IZANAGI'S SPOUSE IZANAMI DIED WHILE GIVING BIRTH TO THE FIRE-GOD KAGUZUCHI, AND IZANAGI CUT THE CHILD INTO THREE PIECES. EACH PIECE BECAME A GOD: KURAOKAMI, KURAYAMATSUMI, AND KURAMITSUHA. ALL THREE WERE REGARDED AS SNAKES OR DRAGONS ASSOCIATED WITH RAIN AND SNOW, AND DWELT IN MOUNTAINS OR VALLEYS.

SEA DRAGONS AND WATER SERPENTS

The Nihongi also describes three serpentine gods of waterways or the sea called Watatsumi no Mikoto, Mizuchi, and Ohowatatsumi no Mikoto. One of these is the subject of a story set in the 67th year of Emperor Nintoku's reign (379 BCE). As we shall see, this story explains the origins of the name of a pool in the Kahashima River.

the pool of agatamori

IN THE PROVINCE OF KIBI, AT A FORK IN THE
KAHASHIMA RIVER, A MIZUCHI (MEANING "WATER-DRAGON")
WROUGHT DESTRUCTION UPON THE REGION THROUGH ITS
POISON, WHICH KILLED MANY—BOTH RESIDENTS AND
TRAVELERS ALIKE. AGATAMORI, A STRONG, FIERCE-TEMPERED
MAN AND ANCESTOR OF THE OMI OF KASA, THREW THREE
CALABASH GOURDS INTO THE FORK, CHALLENGING THE DRAGON.
"IF YOU CAN CAUSE THESE THREE CALABASH TO SINK, THEN
I WILL GO AWAY; BUT IF YOU CANNOT—YOU MIZUCHI,
WHO SPEW UP SUCH DEADLY POISON—THEN I WILL KILL YOU
AND CUT YOU INTO PIECES." THE DRAGON CHANGED INTO A
DEER AND TRIED TO SINK THEM, BUT IT COULD NOT.
AGATAMORI DREW HIS SWORD, LEAPT INTO THE RIVER, AND
SLEW IT. DIVING FURTHER DOWN INTO THE POOL, HE FOUND
A CAVE IN WHICH THERE WAS A TRIBE OF MANY MIZUCHI,
AND HE SLEW ALL OF THEM ALSO. THE POOL BECAME
REDDENED WITH THE DRAGONS' BLOOD. FOR THIS REASON
THE POOL WAS KNOWN EVER AFTERWARDS AS
"THE POOL OF AGATAMORI."

Another story is about a sea dragon called Ohowatatsumi no Mikoto or Toyotamahiko no Mikoto, whose names mean "Sea-Lord" and "Abundant-Pearl-Prince."

OHOWATASUMI HAD A MAGNIFICENT PALACE AT THE BOTTOM OF THE SEA. HIS DAUGHTER, TOYOTAMABIME ("ABUNDANT-PEARL-PRINCESS") TOLD HER FATHER SHE HAD SEEN THE FACE OF A HANDSOME YOUNG MAN NAMED HIKOHOHODEMI REFLECTED IN A POOL BY THE GATES OF THE PALACE AND WISHED TO MEET HIM. HIKOHOHODEMI WAS INVITED TO THE PALACE. HE MARRIED THE PRINCESS AND LIVED THERE FOR THREE YEARS, BUT THEN RETURNED TO THE EARTH. TOYOTAMABIME FOLLOWED HIM, AND HE HAD A HOUSE BUILT ON THE SEASHORE FOR HER RESIDENCE DURING CHILDBIRTH. TOYOTAMABIME ASKED HER HUSBAND NOT TO WATCH WHILE SHE WAS IN THE THROES OF LABOR, BUT BECAUSE HE WAS CURIOUS, HIKOHOHODEMI LOOKED ANYWAY. HE SAW THAT TOYOTAMABIME HAD BECOME A DRAGON; WHEN SHE DISCOVERED HIS SPYING, SHE BECAME ANGRY, WENT BACK TO HER FATHER'S PALACE, AND LEFT HER HUSBAND AND CHILD BEHIND.

URASHIMA AND THE DRAGON KINGS

In the province of Tango, on the southern coast of Japan, there was once a village where, in a small cottage beside a stream, there lived a boy named Urashima. Urashima wanted to become a great fisherman, and so while still a youth he practiced fishing with a hook and a silken line. One day, he set out upon the sea as usual in his small boat and

the DRAGON Gate

the myth of the fish transformed into a dragon draws upon the traditional association of dragons with waterways. in symbolism that is almost the direct opposite of western dragon myths, where the term "slaying your dragons" is used to mean triumph over a difficult or threatening situation, the story of the dragon gate represents transformation into a dragon as the crowning achievement in a person's life or career.

the story, which originated in china, is known widely in japan. it is said golden koi ("carp") may be transformed into dragons by swimming upstream the length of the yellow river, all the way to a mountain waterfall called "the dragon gate." there, the fish gather annually in the pool beneath the waterfall and try to leap over the falls into the calmer current above. many fail, but those that succeed are transformed into magnificent dragons and fly away into the sky. this legend passed into common japanese usage as a proverb which is applied particularly to students and scholars who, when they pass their examinations, are said to have "passed the dragon gate."

Rising dragon and Mount Fuji
IN THIS INK AND GOLD ON PAPER ILLUSTRATION, THE ARTIST SUZUKI KITSU (1796–1858) PLACES A DRAGON AGAINST THE BACKGROUND OF MOUNT FUJI, A POWERFUL SACRED SYMBOL IN JAPAN.

Urashima Taro

THIS SCENE BY AN UNKNOWN ARTIST (C. 1700) SHOWS URASHIMA FISHING AT SEA. IT APPEARS IN A "NARA E-HON," AN OLD JAPANESE PICTURE BOOK.

began to fish. But instead of a fish, Urashima caught a tortoise on his hook. Feeling compassion for the tortoise, and knowing that tortoises are said in legend to live for thousands of years, Urashima removed it gently from his hook and set it free once again into the sea.

Urashima resumed his fishing; the sun was bright, the day was hot, and the gentle breeze and the lapping of the waves against his boat lulled him into a sweet sleep. In his sleep, he heard a gentle voice calling to him, "Urashima! Urashima!" He stood up in his boat and looked in every direction. To his surprise, he saw the tortoise he had caught and set free earlier. To his greater surprise, the tortoise spoke to him clearly in human language and offered to take him to Ryu-kyu, the Dragon King's palace. Urashima agreed, and set himself on the tortoise's back. The tortoise swam across the waves, and though they made great speed through the water, Urashima found that his clothing stayed dry.

THE LAND OF THE DRAGON KING

When they arrived at the palace of the Dragon King, Urashima was welcomed by all manner of fishes and sea-creatures, servants of the Dragon King. Urashima was shown the way into the presence of Princess Otohime and her servant girls, who were seated in splendid robes colored red, gold, and all the hues of sunlight playing upon the ocean waves. Princess Otohime told Urashima that it was she who had appeared to him in the form of a tortoise, and that Urashima had mercifully set free. By testing him in this way, she had found him to be good-hearted and kind, and she offered herself to him, saying that if he took her as his bride, Urashima would live eternally, never growing old, in a land of everlasting summer.

Urashima accepted Princess Otohime as his bride; the two drank the ceremonial wedding cup of saké, and they were serenaded and served many delicacies on coral trays by the servants of the Dragon King. Their honeymoon lasted three days, after which Otohime showed Urashima through her father's splendid palace. It was filled with many wonders, but the greatest marvel of all was the fabulous land surrounding the palace: in that land, all four seasons existed simultaneously. When Urashima looked to the east, he saw cherry trees and plum trees in the full fragrant blossom of spring. In the south, the trees had attained the full green glory of summer. In the west, the leaves were colored orange and red as with fire, while in the north, the land was covered with snow and there was an ice-covered frozen lake.

MEMORIES OF HOME

While he stood astonished, gazing at these wonders, suddenly the memory of the fishing village, his home, and his mother and father came into his mind, and he longed to see them once again. Otohime wept when he told her of his urgent desire to return to his home, and she begged him to stay one more day. Urashima said he must go, but he agreed to leave his wife only for a single day, whereupon he would return to her side. Otohime gave him a precious jeweled box, a "tamate-bako"—the box of the jeweled hand—to remind him of her and their love. Otohime tied a thread of red silk around it and instructed Urashima not to untie the thread or open the box for any reason. Urashima promised, climbed onto the back of a large tortoise, and was transported back again across the sea to the shores near his home.

Miniature water dragon
THIS WATER DRAGON (c. 1870–80) IS A "NETSUKE," A CARVED TOGGLE USED TO ATTACH A SMALL CONTAINER TO THE OWNER'S ROBE. OWING TO JAPAN'S GEOGRAPHICAL LOCATION, ITS DRAGONS ARE CLOSELY ASSOCIATED WITH THE SEA.

歸國浦島

Urashima on the turtle

IN THIS SKETCH BY YOSHITOSHI (1882) URASHIMA RETURNS HOME TO HIS VILLAGE ON THE BACK OF A LARGE TORTOISE. UPON HIS RETURN, HE WILL DISCOVER THAT EACH OF THE THREE YEARS HE WAS AWAY HAD BEEN A CENTURY IN HIS HOMELAND.

Making his way across the beach into the countryside, Urashima found almost everything he remembered had vanished as if it had never been. There were no fishing boats; there was no village, and no trace of his cottage, only the stream which once had flowed beside it. When he asked where he was and what had happened to his beloved home, Urashima was told that a young man had once lived in that place and had drowned at sea while fishing one day; but that was some three hundred years earlier, and all his family—his parents, his brothers and sisters, and their children and grandchildren—had long since passed away also. The young boy's name had been Urashima.

THE BOX OF THE JEWELED HAND

Then Urashima recalled that the Dragon King's splendid palace was believed to be situated in a land where one day was equal to a hundred years. Stricken with sorrow for his beloved family, Urashima made his way weeping back to the seaside as the sun began to set behind the clouds; the seashore began to grow as dark as the gloom in his heart. When he heard the sound of the murmuring sea, he once again remembered Otohime, the Dragon King's Palace, and the marvelous land in which it was set—where the leaves of the trees were like emeralds, the berries like rubies, and where he and his newlywed wife had been attended by the servants of the Dragon King dressed in robes of splendor. The sound of the sea grew louder, and Urashima's heart quickened at the thought that Otohime might be calling to him on the ocean wind. But gazing out upon the sea, the water had grown gray, the waves tipped with splashes of foam. Sadly, there was no welcoming sound of Otohime's voice; no tortoise came to take him back to Ryu-kyu.

Suddenly Urashima remembered the mysterious tamate-bako his bride had given him at their parting. "The box! The box!" Urashima said aloud. "Perhaps there is something inside it that will show me the way back to my wife's side." He untied the red silk thread and slowly lifted the lid of the beautiful box. A little white puff of cloud rolled out from inside the box, lingered for a moment at the edge of the water where Urashima stood, then drifted away upon the ocean wind. Suddenly Urashima found that he was no longer a youth but had become old and wrinkled. His hair had become white and he now had a long white beard blowing in the wind; looking out to sea, he fell forward and collapsed upon the shore. Urashima was dead.

SOURCES: M.W. DE VISSER, THE DRAGON IN CHINA AND JAPAN (1913); ROY BATES, CHINESE DRAGONS (2002); QIGUANG ZHAO, A STUDY OF DRAGONS, EAST AND WEST (1992); F. HADLAND DAVIS, MYTHS AND LEGENDS OF JAPAN (1992).

Indra, Slayer of Vritra

INDRA IS THE GOD OF BATTLES. HE RIDES THROUGH THE SKY, ARMED WITH THUNDERBOLTS, IN A GOLDEN CHARIOT PULLED BY HORSES OF GOLD AND RED. IN THE EARLIEST HINDU MYTHS HE IS NAMED AS THE SUPREME GOD; RULER OF THE ATMOSPHERE; GOD OF RAIN, THUNDER, AND LIGHTNING. INDRA'S EXPLOITS INCLUDE THE RESCUE OF AGNI, THE FIRE GOD, FROM IMPRISONMENT BY THE ASURA, OR DEMI-GODS. INDRA ALSO DESTROYS VALA, A DEMON WHO TAKES THE FORM OF A GREAT CAVERN IN WHICH HE HAS CAPTURED THE SACRED HERDS. IN HIS MOST NOTABLE BATTLE, HOWEVER, INDRA SLAYS THE DRAGON VRITRA, THE MONSTER WHO HAS IMPRISONED THE RAIN AND HELD BACK THE RIVERS.

DRAGON OF THE DEEP

Iconography often depicts Indra as a warrior riding an elephant named Airavata with a thunderbolt and a goad in his hand, with yellow hair and beard. One of the many names given to Indra is Vritrahan, "Slayer of Vritra," a term that has parallels with Verethraghna ("god of victory") in the *Avesta* of Zoroastrianism. He is also called Vajrabhurt or Vajradakshina, "Bearer of the bolt, bearing the bolt in his right hand." Vritra is also named Ahi, "the serpent," and several Vedic hymns praise an obscure deity named Ahibudhnya, "the dragon of the deep."

Later Hindu mythology lists Indra as a Deva, one of the eight guardians of the world. However, more than a quarter of all the hymns in the *Rig Veda* celebrate Indra as the supreme god, even though he shows human weaknesses and vices, and is sometimes punished for his failings.

A GOD IS BORN

Aditi, Indra's mother, carried the god in her womb for a thousand months, and her womb was ripe for the birth of her son. The god, however, did not wish to be born in the normal fashion, and from inside the womb Indra declared: "I shall not be born in the usual way, for I shall be extraordinary in deeds—I will come through your side, mother, and not by the usual path."

The god's mother then said: "You should be born in the normal way, for your coming in that manner will mean my death." In the end, however, Indra was born as a bull from the heifer—stout and strong.

Indra riding an elephant

A MODERN PAINTING, BY INDIAN ARTIST KAILASH RAJ, OF INDRA RIDING HIS GREAT WHITE ELEPHANT AIRAVATA. IN INDIAN MYTHOLOGY, THE SPOTLESS WHITE ELEPHANT IS OFTEN DEPICTED WITH FOUR TUSKS AND SEVEN TRUNKS.

Let the glory of Indra now be proclaimed;
Let us now praise his heroic deeds:
He whose mother walked away from him
is the creator of all, maker of the sun,
wielder of the thunderbolt, slayer of the dragon.
Unconquered conqueror of all,
Indra sliced open the mountains;
He strengthened the earth, lifted up the sky,
freed the herds, released fire.
He slew the dragon, opened up a passage
for the waters.

After Indra's birth, his mother abandoned him, but he followed her to the house of Tvastr. Indra desired the strength of a man, and the strength of bulls, and so he drank three bowls of Soma, the wondrous nectar pressed for him by his comrade Vishnu. Then Tvastr forged for him a mighty thunderbolt. Afterward, Indra slew his father and then set out for a journey of adventure.

THE MIGHTY SERPENT

A mountainous dragon, Vritra, lay upon the uplands, surrounding the waters, encircling and inhabiting them, holding the waters captive. At Indra's approach, the dammed-up waters shrieked shrill as women, crying for release. Muddled and confused, Vritra rose to challenge the god in combat. Armless, legless, handless, and footless, the mighty serpent curled, coiled, lashed head and tail, and struck against the hero. Vritra threw lightning, hail, mist, and thunder. Indra struck back with his hundred-angled golden bolt, his thunderbolt of a thousand points. At Indra's anger, the forger of the mighty weapon, Tvastr, trembled; heaven and earth quaked with the tumult.

But Indra had drunk the potent Soma, drained it down to the bottom of the cup, and his strength was matchless. He hurled his mighty weapon, his terrible thunderbolt, which found its target in Vritra's flanks. Indra Maghavan, "the Generous One," took the thunderbolt forged by Tvastr and cast as a weapon, killing Vritra, the first-born dragon.

SEVEN STREAMS

With his mighty thunderbolt, Indra slew the shoulderless serpent, enclosed the Encloser, split him asunder as a tree-trunk shorn of its branches. The dragon was no match for the mighty warrior, and his head was crushed. Flattened by Indra's stroke, the dragon lay stretched out like a reed shattered in many places; his body lay severed in many pieces. Indra bore down with his weapon, found with the point the dragon's inward parts, and made a way for the pent-up water. With his weapon he carved out channels for the waters to follow, seven streams through which they flowed.

The waters gushed forth, crying out in gladness, lowing like cattle. They ran quickly down to the sea. The waters Vritra had so long encircled, enclosed, enfolded, now flowed freely for mankind's good. The flood rose higher; Vritra lay at the edge of the water; the floodtide belonging to Man swelled, covering the corpse. Then Vritra sank through the watery darkness to a secret place. The seven rivers of Punjab ran free.

No enemy appeared to avenge the dead Vritra; Indra strode then over the seven rivers and the ninety-nine streams. He is king over all creation, over all that moves and all that moves no more, over the wild and the tamed, surrounding all.

Sources: WALTER H. MAURER, *PINNACLES OF INDIA'S PAST: SELECTIONS FROM THE RIG VEDA* (1986); WENDY DONIGER O'FLAHERTY, *THE RIG VEDA* (1981); A. A. MACDONNELL, *THE VEDIC MYTHOLOGY* (1971); RALPH GRIFFITH, *THE HYMNS OF THE RIG VEDA* (1963).

Ra, Set, and Apep

THE DRAGON MYTH OF ANCIENT EGYPT CENTERS ON RA, THE SUN GOD; HIS PROTECTOR SET, THE STORM GOD; AND APOPHIS, OR APEP, A SERPENT LURKING IN THE DARK WATERS OF THE UNDERWORLD. THE SYMBOLIC ROLES OF THIS ANCIENT EGYPTIAN BEAST ARE AMBIGUOUS. IT COULD BE THE PRIMORDIAL SPIRIT OF CREATION, OR A MONSTER OF CHAOS AND DISORDER; LIKE THE CHINESE DRAGON AND THE SERPENTS OF WESTERN MYTH, IT IS SOMETIMES THE COSMIC ENEMY, AND AT OTHER TIMES A FERTILITY SPIRIT.

JOURNEY THROUGH THE UNDERWORLD

The primal serpent's associations with death, disorder, and the dark, watery underworld are particularly evident in the myth of Set, Ra, and Apep. The sun-god Ra makes a nightly journey through the underworld from the sunset mountains in the west back to the land of sunrise in the east. During the twelve hours of the night, as Ra makes his way through the dark waters beneath the earth, he encounters many dragon-like monsters. The largest and most important of these is Apep, who, during the ninth hour, the darkest hour of the night, attacks Ra's vessel in an effort to halt the god's progress. Set and other gods capture and chain him, slay him with spears, and dismember him, guaranteeing Ra's safe arrival in the east and the rising again of the life-giving sun.

At dawn, the sun-god Ra sets sail upon the vast ocean of Nun to light the world. In the morning his boat is called "Matet" (growing stronger), and in the evening "Semket" (growing weaker). Ra sits enthroned mid-deck, Horus sits aft and tends the rudder; the boat is guided by Thoth and Maat (wisdom and truth) and by two fish, Abtu and Ant.

As evening falls, Ra approaches the dark waters of Tuat, the underworld. Tuat is a long, narrow valley through which flows a river. On the sandy banks on either side there are innumerable monsters, fiends, and demons of all kinds and sizes, terrifying to anyone who enters the valley. Their terror is amplified by the deep darkness in which they dwell. Through this valley the vessel of Ra sails through the hours of the night, each hour marked by barriers the god must pass in order to continue his journey.

Journey through the underworld

THIS IMAGE DEPICTING RA, THE MOST CENTRAL GOD IN THE EGYPTIAN PANTHEON, DATES FROM BETWEEN C. 3000 AND 200 BCE. RA APPEARS MID-DECK. EACH NIGHT, HE AND OTHER GODS DO BATTLE WITH DRAGONLIKE MONSTERS.

egyptian myth

though mythic beliefs concerning creation originated in the early dynastic period, most of the sources for egyptian mythology date from the old kingdom period, about the time the great pyramid complexes at giza and elsewhere were created.

✛

SERPENT OF THE DARKNESS

In the FIRST HOUR of the night, the boat enters Tuat through a hall or ante-chamber in which dwell the souls of men and women who died without the benefit of the priestly rituals, who hope to enter the boat and continue their journey. Ra is surrounded by the folds of the huge serpent Mehen, its tail in its mouth. The boat approaches a pillar marking the entrance to the second hour. The doors are closed, guarded by the huge serpent named Saa-Set, standing on its tail.

Ra's boat enters the SECOND HOUR of the night, preceded by the boats of Osiris (the Moon); Isis/Hathor; Anubis and Apuat; and Nepr, god of grain and vegetation. Ra now stands amidships in a shrine, protected by Mehen and another serpent standing on its tail. The gods shout, "Ra shall trample upon the Eater of the Ass, Apep, the Great Serpent of the Darkness."

In the THIRD HOUR, the boat passes a huge serpent lying on top of the shrines of twelve gods of the Lakes of Fire. The serpent god Apep appears, slips into the water, and follows Ra's boat.

DEVOURING THE NIGHT

In the FOURTH HOUR, the region is so dark that Ra's boat itself provides light from a serpent with a head at each end, whose mouths issue fire. This realm is filled with huge snakes and dragons, including Hetch-nau, with a human head at each end. There are serpents with three and four heads, some with human feet and legs. There is Herert, who bears twelve young serpents who devour the twelve hours of night.

In the FIFTH HOUR, Ra's boat passes through the land of Seker, a two-headed, winged serpent god whose tail ends in a human head. The serpent Tepan appears, who takes the daily offerings of the living to Seker, followed by the serpent Ankh-aapau, issuing flames from its mouth. The gods of Ament appear holding a long serpent. Nine gods bear on their shoulders the serpent Ennutchi.

In the SIXTH HOUR, the boat passes by the throne of Osiris, who sits distributing justice. This region contains a house with sixteen rooms containing guardians of a five-headed serpent, Ash-hrau. The three houses of Ra are here guarded by a serpent god standing on its tail, emitting fire from its mouth. There is the serpent-monster Am-khu, who devours the spirits of Ra's enemies overthrown in the underworld.

RENEWING THE EARTH

In the SEVENTH HOUR, Ra's boat passes through the Gate of Osiris. Here the water grows so shallow that the boat cannot float, and the serpent Neha-hra blocks the way. Isis enters the boat, and utters incantations that propel it magically on its way.

SOURCES

BESIDES THE SO-CALLED "PYRAMID TEXTS" RECORDED IN HIEROGLYPHICS ON MONUMENT WALLS AND STELAE, THE PRINCIPAL SOURCES OF EGYPTIAN MYTHOLOGY INCLUDE *THE BOOK OF THE DEAD, THE BOOK OF THE UNDERWORLD, THE BOOK OF EXHALATIONS, FESTIVAL SONGS OF ISIS AND NEPHTHYS,* AND THE BOOKS OF *TRANSFORMATIONS* AND *LAMENTATIONS.* MIDDLE AND NEW KINGDOM REDACTIONS OF THESE WERE OFTEN GARBLED BY CONFUSED SCRIBES.

✝

In the EIGHTH HOUR, Ra is protected by the mighty snake Mehen. Ra calls out to deities who answer him in voices that sound like humming bees, weeping women, moaning men, lamenting bulls, male cats mewing, war cries and shouts of battle, the cry of the divine hawk, and twittering waterfowl. Ra passes twelve enemies who on earth despised the sacred mysteries of Horus and Osiris. They are bound, tied, and burnt to death by the fires breathed out by a huge serpent named Kheti. A shout is heard: "Praise to Ra, who renews heaven with his soul and the earth with his body! We open heaven for thee and make the paths straight."

In the NINTH HOUR, Apep reappears, and the gods are poised to kill the dragon. They cry: "Come to the places of slaughter that thou mayest be slain, for the gods are against thee." They drive their spears into Apep, destroy the serpent Sesi, and prevent the serpent Ai from rising up out of the water to threaten Ra in his boat.

THE EVERLASTING SNAKE

In the TENTH HOUR, a two-headed serpent called Thes-hrau lies before a city called Metched-qat-utebu. Apep is now bound by a chain held by twelve gods, and the whole realm of Tuat, the underworld, resounds with the voice of Apep as he dies. The serpents Uamemti and Ankhi are held by smaller chains, and the double god Horus-Set accompanies Ra, helping him complete his journey toward sunrise.

In the ELEVENTH HOUR, Ra's boat is surrounded by four divine bearers of light and many accompanying gods, who carry the serpent Mehen on their heads toward the eastern sky. Horus stands on the left bank in a country of flaming fire. A huge serpent called "Set of a million years" devours any of Ra's enemies who escape the realm of the eleventh hour. Ra declares that his father Osiris will condemn his enemies to destruction and Horus will cut off their heads, rend their souls and spirits asunder, and cast them into blazing pits. Set, the everlasting snake, will spew flames upon them and they will be cut in pieces. The voices of the slain, the cries and shrieks of their souls nourish the companions of Horus.

A NEW DAWN

The morning stars shout praises to Ra heralding the sunrise. Apep is now chained to the earth by five chains, and with knives and scepters many gods and goddesses complete the annihilation of the monster.

The TWELFTH HOUR of the night is the last, and the way is guarded by the serpent-gods Sebi and Reri. Twelve gods tow the boat, which now enters the body of a serpent. Ra enters as an old god surrounded by complete darkness but comes out through the serpent's mouth into the daylight renewed and youthful again. Ra emerges in triumph from Tuat, his boat floating on the waters of Nun, whose arms are outstretched to receive him.

SOURCES: ROBERT ARMOUR, *GODS AND MYTHS OF ANCIENT EGYPT* (2001); E.A. WALLIS BUDGE, *THE GODS OF THE EGYPTIANS* (1904); R.T. RUNDLE CLARK, *MYTH AND SYMBOL IN ANCIENT EGYPT* (1959).

Bast kills the demon Apep
THIS ILLUSTRATION FROM THE HUNEFER PAPYRUS (C. 1370 BCE) SHOWS THE EGYPTIAN GODDESS BAST (IN THE FORM OF A CAT) PUTTING THE SNAKELIKE DEMON APEP TO DEATH WITH A KNIFE.

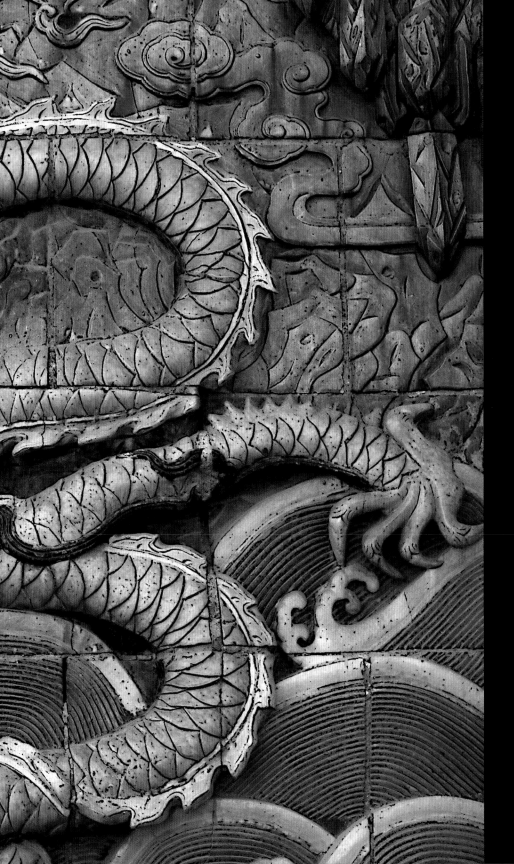

**Detail from the Nine Dragon
Screen, 1771**

This glazed tiled screen located in
the Forbidden City in Beijing, China,
depicts nine writhing dragons playing
with pearls. The number of dragons
symbolizes the emperor's supremacy;
nine is the highest single number.

imperial or divine qualities, many rivers, cities, and mountains have the dragon character as part of their names. For example, one of the largest rivers in Manchuria is the Hei Lung Kiang, or "Black Dragon River," named from a large black dragon that is reputed once to have appeared in it.

THE DRAGON'S APPEARANCE

In very early times, it was thought that dragons should be drawn with a horse's head and serpent's tail. Wang Fu (73–48 BCE) claimed that the dragon's head was more like a camel's, with devil's eyes, ox's ears, scales like a carp, eagle's claws with tiger's soles, and stag's horns. His source may have been the Er Ya Yi, "The Book of Plants and Animals," but though his description has been repeated numerous times since he first gave it, it is far from accurate to say that dragons have been portrayed in a standard way throughout Chinese tradition. Paintings and images of animals such as tigers, alligators, horses, and serpents could be based on observation, but the dragon of course cannot be observed in nature and so no one could say for certain what one looked like.

The Shan Hai Jing, "The Mountain and Water Classic," describes a particular kind of dragon: "Outside of the north sea, north of the red water, there is the Zhang Wei mountain, in which dwells a spirit with a human face and the body of a snake, and red staring eyes. When they close it is dark, when they are open it is light. This spirit does not eat or sleep. He does not breathe. Wind and rain obey his command. He lights up the deepest darkness. This spirit is called the candle dragon." — Roy Bates, *Chinese Dragons*.

THE ORIGINS OF fêNG-SHUI

CHINESE GEOMANCY, OR fêNG-SHUI (LITERALLY, "WIND-WATER"), ORIGINATED IN THE BELIEF THAT FOUR INVISIBLE ANIMALS RESIDING IN THE EARTH — THE BLACK TORTOISE, THE WHITE TIGER, THE GREEN DRAGON, AND THE RED PHOENIX — GOVERNED GOOD OR BAD FORTUNE IN THE HUMAN WORLD. TOMBS, HOUSES, FARMS, AND GARDENS HAD TO BE SITUATED TO TAKE BEST ADVANTAGE OF THESE NATURAL FORCES. THE DRAGON IS ASSOCIATED WITH WATER, SPRING RAINS, LIFE, REBIRTH, AND GOOD FORTUNE.

✝

THE DRAGON BOAT FESTIVAL

The first five days of the fifth month of the year are celebrated in a festival in which the people seek to please the god of rivers, encouraging him to send plentiful rain for the height of the growing season. This festival can be traced back to 295 BCE and may date from even earlier. Its basis is in the following story.

Ch'u Yuan was a beloved statesman in the country of Ying. One of the lesser princes in the country was jealous of Ch'u Yuan and accused him of corruption. Ch'u Yuan was innocent of the charges, and in an act of protest against the falsehood and anger with the corruption into which the state had fallen, he drowned himself in the Mi-lo river. Mourning his loss, the citizens of Ying sent out search parties in boats carved with dragon prows or decorated with dragon images and tried to recover Ch'u Yuan's body.

In the modern festival, flag-draped boats as long as 125 feet from prow to stern are piloted down the river, gongs sounding, carrying specially prepared rice-cakes. The first boat to reach the place where the statesman is thought to have drowned himself is allowed to make the first sacrifice to the memory of Ch'u Yuan.

SOURCES: EDWARD T.C. WERNER, *ANCIENT TALES AND FOLKLORE OF CHINA* (1986); HARRY T. MORGAN, *CHINESE SYMBOLS AND SUPERSTITIONS* (1942); ROY BATES, *CHINESE DRAGONS* (2002); QIGUANG ZHAO, *A STUDY OF DRAGONS, EAST AND WEST* (1992).

> " THE PRIMARY CONCEPT OF THE CHINESE DRAGON FLOATING THROUGH CLOUDS DERIVES FROM CONTEMPLATING THE SKY. BOTH THE SHAPE AND THE MOVEMENT OF THE CHINESE DRAGON ARE SIMILAR TO ROLLING CLOUDS. "
>
> QIGUANG ZHAO,
> *A STUDY OF DRAGONS,*
> *EAST AND WEST*

Baal and Yamm

THE MYTH OF BAAL'S COMBAT WITH YAMM, THE DRAGON-GOD OF THE SEA, IS KNOWN PRINCIPALLY FROM RECORDS INSCRIBED ON CLAY TABLETS EXCAVATED AT THE RUINS OF THE ANCIENT CANAANITE CITY OF UGARIT, NOW RAS SHAMRA IN MODERN-DAY SYRIA. THE RUINS INCLUDED ROYAL BUILDINGS, TEMPLES OF BAAL AND DAGON, AND LIBRARIES CONTAINING THOUSANDS OF TABLETS, ALL DATING FROM APPROXIMATELY 1400 TO 1200 BCE, WHEN THE CITY WAS DESTROYED. BAAL WAS THE MOST IMPORTANT OF THE GODS HONORED AT UGARIT.

. . . .

THE BAAL CYCLE

Bronze-age Ugarit was an important trading center, and people from many different cultures lived there: Egyptians, Babylonians, Hurrians, and Hittites. Some similarities between the Ugaritic religion and those of the other ancient Near Eastern cultures can be found, including parallels with biblical material. The Baal cycle narrates three key events in the life of the god: the construction of his house, or temple, with the consent of the chief god El; Baal's fight with Yamm, the god of the sea described as a dragon; and his fight with Mot, or Death. Since one of the names given to Yamm in this myth is Lotan, many have seen a resemblance between Baal's vanquishing of Yamm and Yahweh's defeat of Leviathan in the Old Testament. Baal's return from the dead after his defeat by Mot may be regarded as an example of the dying-and-rising god motif found elsewhere in ancient mythology and as a prefiguration of the resurrection of Christ in the New Testament.

Blue dragon robe
DETAIL OF A DRAGON ON A 19TH-CENTURY EMBROIDERED SILK ROBE, WHICH FORMED PART OF THE OFFICIAL COSTUME OF THE CHINESE IMPERIAL FAMILY AND ITS OFFICIALS.

Storm god Baal

THE DIVINE BULL

High on Mount Zaphon, the "Mount of Victory" which the Greeks call
Kasios, there was a solemn assembly of the gods. Asherah, Anat, Kothar,
and many others were present before the throne of El, the ancient one,
the divine bull, the father of time, the holy one, creator of the earth and
all the gods. Chief among the younger gods was Baal, the son of Dagon
and cup-bearer to El, a prince known as the "Rider of the Clouds."
Yamm, the god of the sea, was also there; both wanted El to grant them
supreme lordship over all the earth. Baal was young and strong and
seemed likely to receive the throne; but Yamm was El's son, and he was
favored by El. He was a dragon, the god of the sea, also called Lotan.

Yamm came forward before the throne of El and cast himself down in
humility before his father, the elderly god. Then he rose and in a loud
voice he demanded: "Let a house be made for me here on the mountain
of night so that I may be honored over all the earth."

THRONE OF THE GODS

Now El was old. The time of his vigor had long passed. As a weak king, he
had little with which to challenge the brash demand of the powerful sea-
god. El also resented Baal's arrogance in presuming he should succeed to
lordship over his son Yamm. And so he consented to Yamm's wish. But the
goddess Asherah rose quickly in the presence of all and reproved El for
foolishly allowing Yamm to challenge Baal's priority: "In this way, Lord El,
Yamm wishes to claim the high throne of the gods for himself, displacing
thy son." El hesitated, and Yamm withdrew quickly from the assembly.
The gods dispersed, leaving El on his throne, alone with his thoughts.

Sea dragon, 1890

GORDON WAIN'S IMAGINATIVE DEPICTION
OF A DRAGON OF THE SEA ATTACKING A SMA[...]
BOAT. LIKE APEP, WHO BESIEGES RA'S BOAT,
THE MESOPOTAMIAN MONSTER YAMM IS
DESCRIBED AS A TERRIFYING WATER MONSTER[...]

A short time later, however, Yamm sent his two messengers back to the assembly chamber to put his demand to the god with greater force. Before they left, Yamm instructed them:

> " when you face my father el
> before the assembly of gods
> on the mountain of night,
> do not fall before his feet,
> do not lie prostrate before him,
> but stand boldly and declare
> my message, saying:
>
> 'hand over to me baal,
> the son of dagon,
> so that i may gain his
> inheritance as my own,
> the earth and all the gold
> that lies within it!' "

In due time, the messengers of Yamm arrived in the assembly chamber, just as the feast was about to begin. The gods had not yet fully assembled; Baal, El's cup-bearer, stood beside his throne. Yamm's men strode boldly to the throne of El. Standing before him, they stated their lord's demand. This time, they said: Yamm wanted not only a house built in his honor; he also claimed the throne of the earth. But he also demanded that Baal be enslaved as a servant to Yamm forever. Between the folds of their robes, El could see the glint of gold, the flash of blades hidden within their garments.

BANISHED TO THE WILDERNESS

The gods were astonished. Those who were seated hung their heads and averted their eyes from Yamm's messengers in fear of them and their powerful lord, the sea. Baal cried out against the gods, rebuking them for their fear of Yamm and his messengers; he called upon El to refuse Yamm's demands. But El had no strength of will to oppose his powerful son, and so he consented. He instructed the messengers to take back his reply:

> " o yamm, baal shall be thy slave.
> baal shall be thy servant,
> the son of dagon thy prisoner;
> baal shall pay tribute to you as a deity,
> he will bring you gifts as
> the god of the earth. "

Baal, who stood beside El as his server, heard all this; he too had seen the weapons concealed beneath the messengers' robes. He stepped forward quickly, armed with knives, to attack the servants of Yamm. But the goddess Anat and the goddess Asherah leapt up to intervene, one catching the right hand and the other the left hand of Baal before he could strike. They were angry with Baal for so brazen an act of violence in the presence of the king of the gods, angry also that he was tempted to strike down Yamm's servants, who were merely the messengers of the great god of the sea. Asherah blamed him, and El banished him to the wilderness. Baal withdrew in shame; but before he departed, he instructed Yamm's messengers to give their lord this

Baal, 14th century BCE

message: "Baal will never bow to Yamm, nor will he be his slave. I declare that one day I will slay Yamm the tyrant." The messengers left the council; Baal went out in shame and anger. When news of all these things was delivered to Yamm, he gloated within himself.

THE TYRANT YAMM

El commanded Kothar-u-Kasis, the divine craftsman, to build a house for Yamm on the side of Mount Zaphon. Yamm was exultant; he inaugurated his reign with an immense feast in which the gods and goddesses entertained themselves with dancing, filled themselves with fine food, and became intoxicated on enormous amounts of wine. There were many wild celebrations of this kind; but Yamm soon began to rule the others with harsh cruelty. He drove the lesser gods as a tyrant, commanding upon them hard tasks of labor. In exile in the wilderness, Baal was harassed by monsters, some of them with seven heads with mocking faces identical to that of Baal himself.

From the wilderness, Baal could hear the revelries on Mount Zaphon. On one occasion he made his way secretly up to the mountainous heights to spy upon the wild celebrations and to gaze with longing upon the goddesses of El, his former consorts. Another time, he sent a message to his sister Anat, begging her to come to him. She came, and he begged her to intercede with El to commission the construction of a house for Baal to dwell in. Anat agreed. Seeing the resolve in Anat's eye as she drew near, El fled to an inner chamber of the palace. Anat pursued him, and after much threatening the aged king emerged and honored her request, committing the work to Kothar-u-Kasis, the craftsman of the gods.

DEATH THROUGH OPEN WINDOWS

Now Kothar-u-Kasis oversaw the construction of Baal's temple, but when he suggested a window be placed from which Baal could overlook the sea, Baal objected. "Mot," he said, "brings death through open windows." But Baal was also reluctant to provide an opening through which he could be spied upon in his intimacies with the goddesses in his entourage. When the house was completed, it was consecrated with revels even more grandiose than any seen before on Mount Zaphon. Invigorated by the conjugal acts with which he celebrated his success, Baal went out and conquered ninety cities. Then he returned home to his temple.

Yamm continued to reign as cruelly as ever, until Asherah begged him to show some mercy to the other gods, her sons. He refused. Then she offered her own body to the tyrannical ruler, hoping to purchase the gods' release with the pleasure of their conjugal union. To this, Yamm agreed, and a time was appointed for their intimacies to take place.

Asherah returned to the court of El and told her plan to him and the other gods assembled there in council. They consented. When news of this reached Baal in his temple, he was furious: furious that Asherah would offer herself to Yamm and angry that the gods would allow such a deed to take place. He would not agree to her surrendering herself to the tyrant Yamm. So he sent word to the council of El, swearing that he would go forth to do battle with Yamm and destroy him, ending his tyrannical reign forever.

Hearing this, Kothar-u-Khasis formed a plan. He went to Baal and said:

> " O PRINCE BAAL, RIDER OF CLOUDS,
> THOU WILT SMITE THINE ENEMY YAMM,
> VANQUISH MOT THY FOE,
> AND TAKE THE EVERLASTING KINGDOM
> UNDER THINE OWN ETERNAL SOVEREIGNTY FOREVER. "

Then Kothar constructed two clubs for Baal, proclaiming their names.

To the first, which he called Yagrush, "expeller," Kothar said:

> " THOU SHALT EXPEL FROM HIS THRONE YAMM,
> THE DRAGON OF THE SEA,
> DRIVE FROM HIS SOVEREIGN SEAT
> NAHAR, THE DRAGON OF THE RIVERS.
> LIKE A RAPTOR SHALT THOU FLY
> FROM THE HAND OF BAAL
> AND STRIKE YAMM IN HIS MIDDLE. "

The other he named Aymur, "driver," and to it he said:

> " THOU SHALT DRIVE YAMM FROM
> HIS SOVEREIGN THRONE,
> LIKE A RAPTOR SHALT THOU FLY
> FROM THE HAND OF BAAL
> AND STRIKE YAMM BETWEEN THE EYES,
> BETWEEN THE EYES OF NAHAR OF THE RIVERS.
> THEN NAHAR SHALL SINK DOWN;
> YAMM SHALL FALL DEAD
> TO THE DUST OF THE EARTH. "

BAAL THE CONQUEROR

Armed with the weapons, Baal went out to face Yamm. Yamm uncoiled and attacked Baal with his mighty serpentine folds, trying to drag him down into the watery abyss. Baal swung his weapon Yagrush and struck the dragon in the middle of its torso; the dragon was stunned but the thousand joints of its monstrous snaky frame remained intact. Yamm leapt forward in a second onslaught. This time Baal drew Aymur and struck the dragon in the middle of its skull. With a terrible crushing sound of splintering bone, Yamm's head was shattered. The dragon stumbled, fell back, and collapsed to the ground. Its lifeless body lay limp; its skeletal frame collapsed under its own weight, and Yamm lay as a heap of inert flesh.

A shout of victory went up; Astarte cried out in praise of Baal:

> " HAIL TO BAAL! BAAL THE CONQUEROR!
> RIDER OF THE CLOUDS, ALL HAIL!
> FOR YAMM OUR TYRANT IS NOW OUR CAPTIVE,
> LOTAN OUR CAPTIVE IS NOW DEAD! "

All the gods joined in praise of the mighty victor:

> " WHO NOW CAN ARISE AGAINST THE LORD BAAL?
> FOR HE HAS SLAIN THE DRAGON,
> DESTROYED THE WRITHING SERPENT OF THE DEEP,
> LOTAN, THE TWISTING SERPENT.
> BUT BAAL THE LORD LIVES!
> ALL HAIL BAAL! "

SOURCES: N. WYATT, TRANS., *RELIGIOUS TEXTS FROM UGARIT* (1998); MICHAEL DAVID COOGAN, TRANS., *STORIES FROM ANCIENT CANAAN* (1978); JOHN DAY, *GOD'S CONFLICT WITH THE DRAGON AND THE SEA* (1985); ARVID S. KAPELRUD, *BAAL IN THE RAS SHAMRA TEXTS* (1952); SIMON BARKER, TRANS., *UGARITIC NARRATIVE POETRY* (1997).

Marduk, Ti'amat, and the Creation of the World

THE BABYLONIAN CREATION MYTH RECORDED IN THE ENUMA ELISH CENTERS UPON A COSMIC BATTLE BETWEEN THE FORCES OF ORDER AND THE FORCES OF CHAOS, SYMBOLIZED BY MARDUK, THE HERO AND CHAMPION OF THE DIVINE WORLD, AND TI'AMAT, THE GODDESS OF DISORDER, DEATH, AND OPPOSITION TO THE DIVINE PLAN. THE STORY WAS FOUND ON SEVEN FRAGMENTARY CUNEIFORM TABLETS RECOVERED FROM THE LIBRARY OF THE AKKADIAN RULER ASHURBANIPAL IN THE 19TH CENTURY.

. . . .

IN THE BEGINNING

In the *Enuma Elish*, Ti'amat parallels Marduk's other cosmic opponents, Ninurta, Zu, and Labbu. Labbu appears frequently in Mesopotamian art as a composite lion-snake monster; Zu has wings and is seen as a winged dragon; similarly, with horns, a tail, and thick hide suggesting scaly armor, Ti'amat was clearly understood to be a dragon. Echoes of the *Enuma Elish* can be found in the Ugaritic mythic cycle of Baal and, more faintly, in Yahweh's conquest of Leviathan in the Bible. The cult of Marduk was associated with Babylon, whose dragon-slaying god was Bel, with whom the Marduk figure later merged. The title comes from the first two words of the text, which mean "when in the beginning"—an echo of the beginning of the book of Genesis.

THE DIVINE PARENTS

There was a time before time when neither the sky above nor the earth below had been created or named. Neither the reed-beds nor the pasture-lands had yet come to be; nor had Man, nor any of the gods—neither their names nor their fates—come into being. There were only the divine parents: Apsu, the lord of the lakes, the sweet waters, who was called "The First;" and Ti'amat, the goddess of the salt-water sea. She was called "The Begetter" because it was she who brought forth all things. From Apsu and Ti'amat came Mummu, then Lahmu and Lahamu—twins, a brother and sister—also known as Ea and Damkina. They then gave birth to Anshar and Kishar, from whom came Anu the sky god, whose son was Nudimmud, the wisest of the gods.

Ninurta attacking Anzu

ANCIENT NEAR EASTERN MYTHS OFTEN DEPICT THE GODS' COSMIC OPPONENT AS A COMPOSITE CREATURE. IN A RELIEF FROM THE PALACE OF NINURTA IN THE ASSYRIAN CITY OF KALAKH (MODERN NIMRUD, IRAQ), THE MONSTER ANZU IS PART LION AND PART BIRD. LIKE THE BABYLONIAN MONSTER TI'AMAT, ANZU IS SLAIN BY AN ARROW THAT TEARS THROUGH ITS INNARDS. THIS IS A 19TH-CENTURY LITHOGRAPH AFTER THE ANCIENT BAS-RELIEF.

TUMULT AND A PLOT

When the clamorous meetings of the younger gods destroyed the sleep of Apsu and Ti'amat, Apsu loudly proclaimed:

> " BY DAY THE WAYS OF THE YOUNGER
> GODS HAVE BECOME A TORMENT;
> BY NIGHT OUR OFFSPRING'S CLAMOR
> HAS DESTROYED OUR SLEEP.
> I WILL SCATTER THEM ABROAD;
> ONE BY ONE WILL I ABOLISH THEM
> THEN WE MAY RETURN TO DAILY REST
> AND NIGHTS OF SWEET SLEEP. "

Ti'amat objected, "Their revels are troublesome, but we should endure them." But Mummu murmured to Apsu, "End their annoying ways that thou and thy spouse might sleep in peace." Apsu's face grew radiant, pondering revenge against the younger gods.

Their scheming was overheard. When they heard the news, the young gods fell mute. Then Ea devised a plan. He invoked a magic circle to enfold them, then recited an incantation to put Apsu to sleep. Ea removed Apsu's belt, his tiara, and the cloak of his lordship, and put them on. Then he stunned Mummu into a sleepless stupor, bound him, laid him across Apsu, and slew them both.

THE BIRTH OF MARDUK

Ea established a dwelling on top of the slain elder god and called it "Apsu," deriding his vanquished foe. He designed chapels, shrines to his divine self and the other gods, and private rooms. He brought Damkina, his lover, there and they lived together in glory.

Deep within those precincts, the temple's most sacred space, Marduk was begotten by Damkina, fathered by Ea. She nursed him at her breast, filling him with divinity: Marduk was majestic in stature, with flashing eyes and proud bearing. He was exalted above the other gods and blessed with double divinity. With four enormous eyes and ears, Marduk could see and hear all things. Fire flashed from his lips.

TI'AMAT'S REVENGE

Ti'amat mourned day and night over Apsu's death, her heart heaving within her breast. The other gods complained:

> " you said nothing and did less when
> apsu was slain; now the winds torment
> you and disturb our sleep.
> have you no care for mummu
> who also was slain?
> have you no care for your children,
> whose eyes are sunken for lack of sleep?
> proclaim battle; take revenge!
> reduce your enemy to nothing! "

Mushussu dragon

This bronze sculpture of a horned dragon c. 800–600 bce, closely resembles many other images of serpentine monsters in Mesopotamian mythology. Mushussu (meaning "the red/ furious serpent") dragons are among the host of monsters Ti'amat summons into battle against Marduk.

Ti'amat gathered fierce gods; they shrieked and raged, resolved upon war. The mother of all things vicious, she created enormous serpents with razor-sharp teeth and fangs; venom flowed in their veins. She formed horned serpents, mushussu dragons, snakes, lions, and scorpion-men, chanting: "All who see them will quail in terror! They shall show no mercy in battle!" She created her spouse Kingu, chief of the monsters, and set him upon a throne with the Tablet of Destinies granting his word the power of law.

A MIGHTY WEAPON

Ea told Anshar of Ti'amat's war-council, and Anshar fretted, bit his lips and twisted his fingers. He said, "Who has power over Ti'amat but you, who slew Apsu?" Ea argued, "You have the fate of all within your power! Make a mighty weapon, unfathomably strong, against Ti'amat!" Anshar made the weapon of warriors, the kašušu whose stroke cannot be borne; he charged Ea to quell Ti'amat's fury with it.

Ea journeyed toward Ti'amat. But terror of her and her monsters overcame him. He returned to Anshar, saying she was too fierce to face in battle. Anshar shook his head and gnashed his teeth in anger. Nudimmu then was charged to fight Ti'amat. He went toward her, but fear overcame him, too, and he returned to Anshar. "She is too fierce to face in battle," he said. Anshar gnashed his teeth again in anger. The gods cried out: "Who will arise and face our foe?"

MARDUK THE HERO

From his secret dwelling, Ea called forth the perfect-hearted peerless one, the gods' mighty heir, their champion: Marduk the Hero! Marduk went before Anshar's throne and said: "Rejoice! Soon your foot shall rest upon the neck of Ti'amat, who will lie dead at your feet! But proclaim me Master of Fate: say that I—not you—shall rule the destinies." The gods agreed: Marduk would be their champion, honored among them as the greatest of gods. They gave him the Kishat-kal-gimreti, "the Royal Scepter."

Marduk rode a chariot of storm drawn by two teams of horses—"Slayer," "Merciless," "Trampler," and "Flyer;" and "Open-lipped," "Ignorant-of-Weariness," "Battle-fierce," and "Relentless Subduer." He carried a mace, a bow, and a quiver; he filled himself with flame and cast lightning before him. Marduk was covered with armor; his lips held an enchantment and his hand a herb against poison. The gods' champion set forth to battle.

Babylonian carvings

BECAUSE HE WAS MOST RENOWNED FOR HIS DEFEAT OF THE DRAGON TI'AMAT, MARDUK'S SYMBOL WAS THE DRAGON. BABYLONIAN ARCHEOLOGY IS REPLETE WITH SCULPTURES, CARVED RELIEFS, AND STATUES OF DRAGONS. AS ILLUSTRATED BELOW, THE MYTHOLOGY DIFFERENTIATED BETWEEN HORNED SERPENTS AND LION-DRAGONS. BOTH SYMBOLIZED DIVINE POWER OVER DESTRUCTIVE COSMIC FORCES.

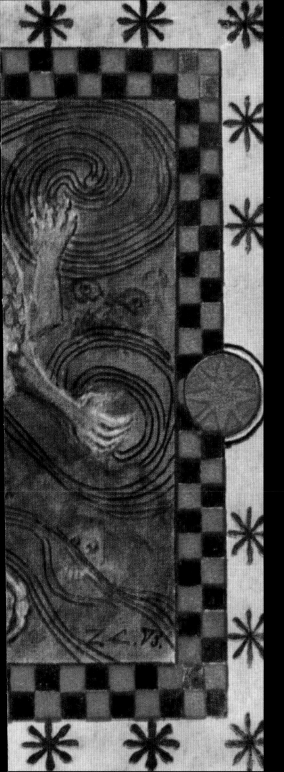

THE THREE WINDS

Marduk drew near. Ti'amat's forces surrounded him. Seeing her monstrous battle-array, his heart quailed; his resolve melted. Seeing fear in Marduk's face, the faces of his companions fell in dismay. Ti'amat wove a deceitful spell, flattering Marduk, praising his strength, wooing him to her. But Marduk recited a litany of her evils and deflected her lies. He challenged Ti'amat to single combat. Calling upon Tempest, Whirlwind, and Tornado to hem her in, he encircled Ti'amat in a net. Ti'amat shook with rage, shrieked aloud; her insides churned.

They met in combat. She opened her mouth to swallow him, but the three winds kept her lips open and inflated her belly. Marduk shot an arrow through her mouth. It tore through her heart. Ti'amat died.

Marduk cast down her corpse and stood upon it in triumph. Her forces scattered. He turned and killed Kingu, turned again and trampled Ti'amat's lower body, then shattered her skull. He split asunder her monstrous form; with half he fashioned the sky, bolted and barred to hold it aloft. With the other half he made earth, opened her ribs right and left as gates for the sun. Her spittle became rain-clouds; her nostrils, breasts, and tail became the mountains, valleys, and caverns. Through her eye-sockets flowed the two rivers. He drew out her knotted insides, uncoiled them, and laid them across the ruins of Apsu. Then he said:

Ninurta the charioteer attacks Anzu
THE ICONOGRAPHY OF ANZU ANTICIPATES THE MEDIEVAL
HERALDIC DEVICE OF THE "RAMPANT," OR RAMPAGING,
DRAGON OR GRIFFIN.

> " I WILL Have a GLORIOUS DWELLING MaDe,
> a CENTER of WORSHIP FOR MY PRIVATE QUARTERS.
> THERE THE GODS MAY REST WHEN THEY
> DESCEND FROM THE SKY. ITS NAME WILL
> BE CALLED BAB-ILI, 'THE GATE of GOD.' "

IN PRAISE OF MARDUK

For a full year, bricks were fired for the temple of Esharra; Babylon was built for the worship of Ellil, Anu, and Ea, a dwelling for the gods.

Marduk cast Ti'amat's monstrous brood into the sky for eleven constellations; their images on the temple doors were signs of his lordship. The gods praised him, kissed his feet, bowed before him; they robed him in royal garments, set him on a throne with a kingly crown. They placed a mushussu dragon beneath his feet and a staff of peace at his side.

Marduk was praised with the Fifty Divine Names. May they be remembered forever; may elders explain them to the younger; the wise, the fathers, the shepherds teach them to the learned, the sons, the herdsmen. May Marduk's land be fertile, his commands unaltered.

Let the recitations of the old men which the scribe wrote down be read in days to come, weaving a tale that calls to remembrance the story of Marduk, slayer of Ti'amat.

SOURCES: THORKILD JACOBSEN, "MESOPOTAMIA," IN *BEFORE PHILOSOPHY: THE INTELLECTUAL ADVENTURE OF ANCIENT MAN,* ED. HENRI FRANKFORT ET AL. (1946; RPT. 1973); HENRIETTA MCCALL, *MESOPOTAMIAN MYTHS* (1990); D. WINTON THOMAS, ED., *DOCUMENTS FROM OLD TESTAMENT TIMES* (1958).

the fifty names of marduk

the fifty divine names of marduk listed in the *enuma elish* probably combine epithets describing attributes of the god himself with names of other deities worshipped in babylon and in cultures conquered or annexed by the babylonians. not all of them can be deciphered. some of them are:

addu—"canal-controller"

agilima—"the lofty"

asare—"bestower of ploughland"

bel—"the lord"

e-sizkur—"house of prayer"

ea—god of fresh water, wisdom, and incantation

enbilulu—"protector of canals"

enkurkur—"lord of the lands"

gish-numun-ab—"creator of people"

gugal—"canal-controller"

hegal—"abundance"

lugal-dimmer-ankia—"king of the gods of heaven and earth"

lugal-durmah—"bond of gods"

malah—"boatman"

marutukku—"help of country, city, and people"

mershakushu—"fierce and considerate, furious and merciful"

namru—"pure god who purifies our path"

neberu—"crossing-place"

suhrim—"uprooter of the foe"

zahrim—"destroyer of enemies"

zisi—"silencer of the aggressor"

Marduk, principal deity of Babylon

A carved relief dating from the Kassite dynasty (c. 1800–1200 bce) associates a Babylonian king with Marduk the dragon slayer.

western DRAGONS

Fight between a dragon and a lion
AN EVIL DRAGON ATTACKS A LION IN
THIS DRAWING BY LEONARDO DA VINCI
(1452–1519).

western dragon mythology

Knight fighting a dragon
IN THIS 12TH-CENTURY FRENCH
ILLUSTRATION, A HEROIC KNIGHT
PREPARES TO SLAUGHTER A DRAGON.

In contrast to ancient Chinese and Japanese dragons, which normally represent divine protective and life-sustaining values, dragons in Western mythology are almost universally evil. Much of this symbolism originated in the Mesopotamian and Near-Eastern myths of Apep, Vritra, Yamm, and Ti'amat discussed in the first part of this book. But in the European and Mediterranean tradition—from the ancient Greek myths of Zeus, Apollo, Jason, and Cadmus to medieval stories of saints and heroes—dragons generally symbolize the destructive force of specific sins, vices, or negative attributes. In mythic terms, they play the narrative role of antagonist against divine, semi-divine, or human combatants.

In Western myth, the dragon is almost always imagined as the primordial cosmic enemy, and the story of the hero's great battle against a dragon is regarded by modern scholars as forming the essential plot of a fundamental narrative pattern.

Yvain, the knight with the lion
THIS 15TH-CENTURY FRENCH MINIATURE
PORTRAYS A KNIGHT FIGHTING A DRAGON
WITH THE ASSISTANCE OF A LION.

At the deepest level, this narrative tradition is about conflict. Who can imagine a story without conflict? Even modern stories of the most trivial kind involve an encounter between protagonists and antagonists, and this reflects the essential mythic pattern found in stories of combat between cosmic forces of order and of chaos. Linguists and mythologists including Calvert Watkins and Joseph Fontenrose see the dragon myth as the most enduring manifestation of this pattern, calling it the "ur-myth"—the fundamental mythic plot—of Western civilization. Symbolically, since dragons exist there have to be dragon-slayers.

St. George

Cadmus, Netherlands School, 1497

(FAR RIGHT) IN GREEK MYTHOLOGY, CADMUS KILLED A DRAGON AND PLANTED ITS TEETH; FROM THE TEETH SPRANG A RACE OF FIERCE MEN.

In *Before Philosophy: The Intellectual Adventure of Ancient Man* (1967), the eminent Egyptologist Henri Frankfort calls myth "a form of poetry which . . . proclaims a truth." What truth does the dragon myth proclaim? If the dragon fight is the story underlying Western mythology, the "story of stories," so to speak, what is this story about? Fontenrose sees the Western dragon myth as the expression of an essential cosmic dualism, an eternal struggle between the forces of Eros and Thanatos—life and death. According to this scheme, the dragon is a symbol of chaos, destruction, inaction, and death, which the divine hero opposes with the forces of creation, life, activity, and order.

Curiously, although in many respects they stand in stark contrast, ancient Eastern dragon myths affirm the same idea as the Near-Eastern and Western myths. The creation of the ordered world of human habitation depends upon the power of divine forces to oppose, contain, and defend against supernatural evil. And the same divine power that created the world and gave it life is also necessary for its ongoing survival.

This pattern can be seen in the earliest Western myths of Zeus, Apollo, Jason, Perseus, and Cadmus. It also lies behind later mythic traditions of saints including St. Samson and St. George, and the secular heroes of medieval epic, saga, and romance. Of particular note is the prehistoric tradition of the Germanic myths, where dragons frequently embody vices that threaten to undermine the ordered structures of tribal life.

The dragons fought by Sigurd, Beowulf, Frotho, and many others symbolize greed. In societies without elaborate economic systems of capital and currency, where whole dynasties and tribal cultures depended

upon the free exchange of heirlooms, weapons, and other valued objects, the social harm caused by withholding these things from circulation could be catastrophic. Long before the medieval Church developed the system of Seven Deadly Sins—with avaritia, "avarice," among them—prehistoric societies recognized this threat. We can read these dragon stories as expressions of an underlying myth whose purpose was to expose the monstrosity involved when a ruler turns miserly and hoards greedily acquired treasures instead of generously sharing them.

The story of Sigurd and Fáfnir highlights this. In this legend, the moral horror of murderous greed appears in concrete form, when Fáfnir literally becomes a dragon because of his uncontrolled desire for wealth. In Beowulf, the thief who stirs the sleeping dragon by stealing from its hoard starts a process that leads ultimately to the end of its— and Beowulf's—kingdom.

Medievalist Jacques le Goff sees one of the essential characteristics of the Western dragon myth to be the connection between the dragon-slayer and the liberation of a particular place from supernatural forces of chaos so that human beings may enter and occupy it in peace and safety. Whether the dragon is thought of in religious terms as the enemy of the God of the Bible, or in secular terms as the enemy of the tribe, kingdom, or state, the pattern holds. Although in the myth the god ultimately conquers his cosmic enemy, in the human world the struggle is played out again and again, with the hope of victory always overshadowed by the possibility of defeat.

At the beginning of the modern period, in *The Faerie Queene* (1596), Edmund Spenser published perhaps the most electrifying description of a dragon fight in literature. No narrative of the slaying of a dragon since the tenth-century Beowulf quite compares to Spenser's account of the cataclysmic fight in which the "monstrous, horrible, and vast" dragon "with wrath, and poyson, and with bloudy gore" puts the Redcrosse Knight to his greatest challenge. The forty-seven closely written stanzas of Spenser's poem summed up the whole mythic tradition of dragons—Asian and European, religious and secular—from the most ancient times to the end of the Middle Ages. Spenser outdid them all in sheer narrative force and in the vivid details that portrayed the monster's ferocity while it was alive, and its threat even after its death.

But Spenser's was the last really great dragon in western literature, and the Renaissance authors could be said to have effectively killed off the monster as a viable part of a serious story. The dragon in *The Faerie Queene* represented the culmination of developments in the Western dragon myth, but it also spelled the end of a tradition. Not until Smaug in J.R.R. Tolkien's *The Hobbit*, or Glaurung in *The Silmarillion*, would anyone be his rival.

Zeus and Typhon

THE STORY OF ZEUS AND HIS TITANIC BATTLE WITH TYPHON CAN BE RECONSTRUCTED FROM A VARIETY OF SOURCES, INCLUDING HESIOD'S *THEOGONY*, HYGINUS'S *FABULAE*, *THE HOMERIC HYMNS*, OVID'S *METAMORPHOSES*, AND PLUTARCH'S *ISIS* AND *OSIRIS*. ELEMENTS OF THE MYTH HAVE PARALLELS IN NEAR EASTERN MYTHS AND LOCAL LEGENDS, AND PLUTARCH EMPHASIZES THE SIMILARITIES BETWEEN TYPHON AND THE PRIMAL SERPENT IN EGYPTIAN MYTHOLOGY. LIKE MANY DRAGONS IN BOTH EASTERN AND WESTERN MYTHOLOGIES, TYPHON IS A COMPOSITE MONSTER; IN PART A MYTH ABOUT THE FOUNDING AND STRUCTURE OF THE PHYSICAL WORLD, IT ALSO INCLUDES SYMBOLIC EXPLANATIONS FOR SEVERAL NATURAL PHENOMENA, INCLUDING THE ERUPTIONS OF MOUNT ETNA.

OLYMPIAN BATTLES

At the climax of ten years of war with the Olympian gods, a gigantic battle occurred in which the Titans were defeated and were cast down through a chasm into Tartarus, falling for a full year until they hit the bottom. Then the Giants came forth, brought into being by Earth. They strove to reach the heights of Mount Olympus by tearing the mountains up by the roots and piling them one upon the other until they had reached the summit. All the gods fought against them, most successfully Zeus with his thunderbolts, and Herakles with his arrows. Herakles slew the captain, Alcyoneus, and one by one they were all destroyed.

TYPHON ATTACKS

Zeus conceived bright Athena as the child of his thought. Hera was furious, and in her fury she drew apart from Zeus and called upon the gods. Slapping the ground in her fury, she asked them to grant her a child apart from Zeus who would be his equal in strength. The gods answered, and for a year Hera avoided the bed of Zeus until she brought forth Typhon, who was nursed by Delphyne, the dragon mate of Python. Typhon crawled out from Tartarus and came out upon the earth from the caves of Cilicia, terrifying to look upon. In the fullness of his growth, when he stood upon the earth his head touched the sky and his arms stretched from east to west. While his body was human, a hundred heads in serpent form grew from his shoulders, with fire surrounding them and flashing from their eyes. Typhon had wings, and legs like enormous serpents. Spouting fire, he attacked Mount Olympus. Many of the gods fled, some to hide in the deserts of Egypt, some in the Nile River.

ZEUS FIGHTS BACK

Zeus met his attack with thunderbolts, and Typhon staggered backwards to Syria. Zeus drew an adamantine blade shaped like a sickle and began to wound Typhon, but Typhon wrapped his coils around Zeus, seized the sickle, and cut out the muscles from Zeus's arms and legs. He cast the god's mutilated body into the caves of Cilicia, and set Python's mate,

The monster Typhon
In this 16th-century woodcut, Typhon appears as a fish- or serpent-tailed creature. He was said to be so tall that his head touched the skies.

Delphyne, to guard them. Hermes, however, stole secretly into the caves and recovered the pieces of Zeus' arms and legs and reassembled him. Zeus came out of the caves stronger than ever, throwing lightning bolt after lightning bolt at Typhon, who answered back by uprooting the crust of the earth and chunks of glowing rock from below, hurling them back at the god.

MOUNTAINS OF BLOOD

Typhon began to lose the battle, and staggered back eastward, retreating first to Mount Nyssa, and then to the mountains of Thrace. As Typhon ripped up the mountains and threw them at Zeus, Zeus met each one with a thunderbolt, and they fell back upon Typhon. One, Mount Haemus, "Blood Mountain," was so called because in falling upon the wounded monster's body, it became saturated with his blood. Typhon was mortally wounded by one of Zeus's bolts, and lay stretched out upon the surface of the Mediterranean. Zeus piled rock and earth upon him, making the island of Sicily. Typhon lay beneath the island face up; when the monster in his agonies shifted or moved his shoulders, the Earth quaked; since his mouth was beneath Mount Etna, from time to time it erupted with Typhon's fiery breath. Hephaestus established his smithy there and the dragon's fire provided heat for his forge. There Typhon lay for many a long age.

Fantasy map of a flat earth
BEFORE EXPLORERS CROSSED THE OCEANS IN THE LATE MIDDLE AGES, SOME EUROPEANS BELIEVED THE EARTH WAS FLAT AND THAT DRAGONS HID IN THE DEPTHS OF THE SEA, WAITING TO ATTACK UNSUSPECTING TRAVELERS.

SOURCES: THIS VERSION OF THE MYTH IS ADAPTED FROM SUMMARIES AND RECONSTRUCTIONS OF THE ORIGINAL SOURCES COMPILED AND TRANSLATED IN RICHMOND Y. HATHORN, *GREEK MYTHOLOGY* (1977); H.J. ROSE, *A HANDBOOK OF GREEK MYTHOLOGY* (1928); TIMOTHY GANTZ, *EARLY GREEK MYTH* (1993), WITH OCCASIONAL REFERENCE TO EDITIONS AND TRANSLATIONS OF THE ORIGINAL AUTHORS IN THE LOEB CLASSICAL LIBRARY.

Apollo and Python

THERE ARE SEVERAL VERSIONS OF THE MYTH OF APOLLO'S FIGHT WITH PYTHON. IN THE EARLIEST, *HOMERIC HYMN THREE*, APOLLO GOES TO FOUND A SHRINE AND ORACLE AT PYTHO; WHILE DIGGING THE FOUNDATIONS, HE ENCOUNTERS A FEMALE DRAGON WHOM SOME CALL DELPHYNE, WHO HAD BEEN AFFLICTING THE LAND. HE FIGHTS AND KILLS HER. IN OTHER, FULLER ACCOUNTS, INCLUDING THAT IN OVID'S *METAMORPHOSES*, APOLLO ARRIVES AT DELPHI AND ENCOUNTERS THE DRAGON CALLED PYTHON, GUARDIAN OF THE SHRINE OF GE OR OF THEMIS, WHO BARS HIS WAY TO THE SACRED VALLEY. APOLLO FIGHTS THIS DRAGON, SLAYING IT WITH A HUNDRED OR A THOUSAND ARROWS, AND TAKES POSSESSION OF THE SHRINE OF THE ORACLE AT DELPHI.

THE MYTHS ABOUND

Another version of the myth appears in *Euripides*. While Leto, his mother, is carrying the infant Apollo in her arms towards Delphi, Python—sent, some say, by Hera to punish Leto for sleeping with her husband, Zeus—sees and attacks mother and son. Though still an infant (in some versions only four days old) and still in his mother's arms, the young Apollo shoots arrows, protecting his mother. In some versions, Python is killed, while in others he is only driven away, permitting Leto to escape to Delos, whereupon Apollo returns later to Delphi to exact his revenge.

In yet another version by Ephoros and Pausanias, the dragon Python, also called Drakon, is ravaging the land of Delphi. Apollo, who is en route from Athens to Delphi, intending to bring civilization to the world, is sent for by the people of Delphi to help them against the monster. Apollo comes and kills it.

Hesiod's *Theogony* describes a monstrous serpent that guards the golden apples that lie in sacred places throughout the earth; similarly, the dragon that appears in the Homeric *Hymn to Apollo*—the earliest Greek poem to mention Apollo's monstrous opponent—also acts as a guardian. The poem says that while he is laying the foundations for the temple consecrated to his worship at Delphi, the god encounters a drakaina, a bloated female dragon accustomed to doing great harm to those in the lands around, who guards the spring. Apollo slays the dragon with an arrow, and with great gasps, much writhing and rolling in agony, the dragon dies, and immediately rots to nothing.

CREATION STORY

Before the beginning there was chaos. All the elements contended against each other until at last, whether by the agency of a god or of nature herself, the elements separated. The air, being lighter, rose up, while the earth, made of a heavier substance, sank down until it floated on the primordial waters.

The mountains rose up above the plains, the rivers found their courses, and the earth became fair and bountiful. At that time the Titans occupied the earth, and Epimetheus was charged by them with the

The God Apollo
APOLLO WAS WORSHIPPED AS A SUN GOD, AND BY KILLING THE PYTHON HE EXEMPLIFIED THE MYTHIC DEFEAT OF DARKNESS BY THE POWER OF LIGHT.

creation of a new race of creatures to be called Man. Epimetheus set to work and created all the animals, including Man, and endowed each with its own powers, abilities, and special attributes.

But when he had finished this work, he had no gift to bestow upon Man. And so, with the help of Athena, his brother Prometheus took fire from the sun and brought it back to earth for the benefit of humankind. With the gift of Prometheus, men could now warm themselves, cook their food, and smelt the ores of the earth into pure gold and silver.

THE GIFT OF FIRE

All the other beasts of the earth were at enmity with Man, but now, with the gift of fire, Man could defend himself against the hostile animals. With fire, however, Man could also make weapons, and as a result of misuse of the gift, men became greedy and selfish. Men began to lay claim to lands and possessions. Jealous, they began making war over them. Zeus was enraged. He sought to put an end to this; summoning a council of the gods, he declared he would destroy the earth and create a new race to take the place of Man. Zeus realized that if he set the earth on fire with his lightning, the blaze could rise as high as the heavens themselves and destroy the very abode of the gods. Therefore, he sent floods of rain instead; Poseidon, his brother, released the water of the rivers, caused the oceans to break their bounds, and the whole earth was flooded. All was destroyed, save Mount Parnassus, which towered above the flood.

When the waters receded, everything was covered with fertile soil, and many things grew. Among them grew the enormous serpent Python, who lived underground in the caves beneath Parnassus.

House of the Vettii, Pompeii
FRESCO PAINTINGS DEPICTING MYTHIC SCENES ARE AMONG THE ARTEFACTS PRESERVED BY THE VOLCANIC ERUPTION (79 CE) AT POMPEII. APOLLO'S VICTORY OVER THE PYTHON WAS A FAVORITE SUBJECT.

THE GREAT SHE-DRAGON

Apollo, the son of Zeus and Leto, was banished to the rocky isle of Delos. From there he went to the forest of Crisa, which lay beneath Mount Parnassus, and found an open glade in the forest beneath a rocky cliff. He decided to build a temple to house an oracle for the benefit of all men who should come seeking wisdom and guidance.

And so he measured out the dimensions of the temple and had stones laid for the foundations. The laborers grew thirsty and went in search of water. A spring flowed nearby which was sacred to Telphusa. Its waters were sweet, but within it there dwelled Python, the monstrous dragon. Bloated with age and evil, she had wrought great harm and bloodshed, killing both sheep and men. The great she-dragon was the doom of any who came near her. The laborers returned to the glade and told Apollo of the dragon haunting the spring, and Apollo went to see.

DEATH OF THE SERPENT

As he drew near, the dragon rose out of the cave beneath the spring and closed in for her attack. Apollo fitted an arrow to his bow, drew it back, and let it fly with swift and violent force. The arrow found its mark in her serpentine entrails. Python shrieked and writhed, gasping for breath, knotting and coiling her huge serpent's folds. Her hideous roaring echoed in the woods. Standing over her, Apollo cried, "No longer shall you trouble men in this place! May you rot into the ground! Neither the Chimaera nor your monstrous mate Typhon can save you, for here you shall rot; the soil that gives life to men shall take you until you have become nothing."

With a great issue of blood, Python gave up her life; her writhing ceased, and she was still. She lay only a moment in the hot sun, and in the next moment she began to decompose with such speed that soon there was nothing left but a foul stench. For this reason the place is still called by men "Pytho," which means "rotten." Apollo bears the epithet "Pythian" in honor of the deed.

Apollo slaying Python

IN SLAYING PYTHON, APOLLO USED AN ARROW, A SYMBOLIC COUNTERPART TO THE LIGHTNING BOLTS OF ZEUS AND OTHER ANCIENT MYTHIC FIGURES.

SOURCES: THIS RETELLING OF THE MYTH IS BASED UPON TRANSLATIONS OF HESIOD'S *THEOGONY* AND *HOMERIC HYMN THREE TO PYTHIAN APOLLO*, H.G. EVELYN-WHITE, TRANS., HESIOD, *HOMERIC HYMNS, EPIC CYCLE, HOMERICA* (1914).

Cadmus and Jason

THE TWO MYTHS RETOLD IN THIS CHAPTER ARE CLOSELY RELATED: THE TEETH THAT JASON SOWS IN THE GROUND, WHICH SPROUT AS SPARTAN WARRIORS, CAME FROM THE DRAGON SLAIN BY CADMUS. CADMUS ALSO FEATURES IN AN ANCIENT BABYLONIAN OR SYRO-HITTITE MYTH IN WHICH THE GOD OF THE SUN SEARCHES FOR THE GODDESS OF THE MOON. IN THIS VERSION, CADMUS REPRESENTS THE SUN, AND THE LOST EUROPA BY THE MOON-MARKED COW. CADMUS WAS MARRIED TO ARES'S DAUGHTER HARMONIA; AFTER A LONG LIFE TOGETHER, TROUBLED BY MISFORTUNE AMONG HIS CHILDREN AND GRANDCHILDREN, IT IS SAID THAT CADMUS AND HARMONIA WERE BANISHED TO ILLYRIA, WHERE THEY WERE TRANSFORMED INTO SERPENTS. UPON DEATH, THEY WERE TRANSPORTED TO THE ELYSIAN FIELDS BY ZEUS.

CADMUS AND THE QUEST

Cadmus was one of the three sons of Agenor, King of the Phoenicians. The other two were Phoenix and Cilix. When Agenor's daughter Europa was carried off by Zeus, Agenor ordered the three to go in search of their sister and not to return until they had found her. All three sons departed upon the quest; it was destined, however, that none would succeed in fulfilling the task, and none would ever return to their father.

Cadmus journeyed from Thrace to Greece, going immediately to Delphi to ask for help from Apollo. There, the oracle instructed him to give up his quest to find Europa. Instead, he was told to take the first living thing he saw upon emerging from the temple as his guide. He was to follow it until it lay down to rest. There, he was to sacrifice the animal and on that same spot he was to found a city with wide streets. "Upon doing this, O Blessed Cadmus, you will become famous among men and you shall become a member of the Immortal Ones."

THE COW AND THE DRAGON

When Cadmus emerged from the temple, his eyes first fell on a cow; on each flank it had white markings in the shape of the moon. Summoning his companions, he started out on his journey from Phocis, following the cow for a long time. Finally, in the Aonian Plain in Boeotia, the weary cow lay down to rest. Cadmus began the preparations for the animal sacrifice; spying a spring, he ordered his companions to fetch water for the rituals.

When his companions got there, they found the spring was guarded. A dragon, sacred to the war-god Ares, and perhaps sprung from Ares himself, watched over the water source, and as they drew closer, the dragon lashed out and slew them all. After some time, wondering what had become of his companions, Cadmus went down to the spring himself; there he saw the mangled bodies of his dead companions.

Then he saw the dragon, which attacked him just as it had attacked the men before. But Cadmus fought the dragon valiantly, finally dealing it its death-blow.

Dragons' teeth

THE TEETH DRAWN FROM THE DRAGON OF COLCHIS, SOWN IN SEPARATE ADVENTURES BY JASON AND CADMUS, SPRANG UP AS THE FIERCE SPARTOI, OR "SOWN MEN." THIS DETAIL IS FROM THE PAINTING *CADMUS SOWING THE DRAGON'S TEETH* BY PETER PAUL RUBENS (1577–1640).

THE FOUNDING OF THEBES

Athena, who had been watching the whole episode unfold, appeared to Cadmus and told him to take out the dragon's teeth and sow half of them in the earth of the Aonian Plain as if they were seeds of corn. Athena kept the other half, and later gave them to King Aeetes of Colchis. Cadmus did so, and immediately the teeth sprouted up in the form of armed men. These became known as the "Spartoi," or "sown men."

Cadmus threw stones at these men, causing each one to think that he had been attacked by another of the Spartoi. Thereupon, they began to fight and slay one another; this battle went on until only five were left. These five placed themselves under Cadmus's command and with their help, Cadmus founded the city of Thebes, constructing an acropolis on the spot where the cow had first lain down. The five surviving Spartoi were the progenitors of the noble families of Thebes.

THE MYTH OF JASON

Pelias and Neleus, twin sons of Poseidon, quarreled over who should be king of their city. They separated, going to different places—Neleus to Pylos, and Pelias to the city of Iolcus in Thessaly. There he took the throne of his half-brother Æson, claiming he merely wished to hold it until Æson's infant son Jason was old enough to assume kingship.

Perceiving Pelias's treachery, Jason's mother escaped by night into the mountains, taking her infant son with her. She gave Jason to Chiron, a good centaur, asking him to rear her child. Chiron taught Jason many

Cadmus about to attack a dragon
THIS PEN AND INK DRAWING BY HENDRIK OLTZIUS (1558–1617) PORTRAYS CADMUS ABOUT TO SLAY THE DRAGON THAT HAD JUST SLAUGHTERED HIS COMPANIONS.

things, but the boy responded most readily and skillfully to instruction in the subject of the healing powers of various herbs and plants. Jason's name means "healer."

At the age of 20, Jason returned to Iolus to claim the throne. There he found the city in the midst of a feast honoring Poseidon. Jason was admired by all for his manly beauty and exotic garments; he went to Pelias and demanded his father's throne in exchange for the kingdom's flocks of cattle and sheep. "You may have the throne," said Pelias, "if you accomplish this task: go to the Island of Colchis. There you will find a golden fleece of a ram hanging on a tree. Bring it to me, and the throne will be yours."

ADVENTURES OF THE ARGONAUTS

Jason agreed to Pelias's bargain. At Corinth he had a fifty-oared ship constructed by Argus; he called it "Argo," naming it after the shipwright and the city that he was from. He sent summons far and wide throughout Greece and gathered a crew of valiant warriors—among them was Herakles. The adventures of this crew, the "Argonauts," would be many and various, and many stories are told of their exploits.

Jason and his men set sail upon the Aegean Sea. They landed first at the island of Lemnos, escaping the murderous women there; next they docked in Thrace and rescued Phineas from the Harpies. They sailed through the clashing rocks of the Symplegades and past the land of Amazons to an island of bronze-winged birds. Leaving there, at last they arrived at the island of Colchis in the farthest east of the Black Sea.

Jason and several of his men disembarked and went inland to search for the palace of Aeetes. Passing a forest of willow trees, where the islanders were accustomed to hang the corpses of the dead, they entered the courtyard of Aeetes's palace. There four springs flowed with wine, milk, oil, and warm water. They made their way to Aeetes's throne and Jason told him his story.

THE DRAGON'S TEETH

Learning that the goal of their quest was the Golden Fleece, Aeetes was suspicious. He said he would divulge the location in return for the fulfilment of two tasks: using a team of fire-breathing bulls with bronze mouths and brass hooves, Jason must plow a furrow in the Plain of Ares. If he completed that, he must next sow the furrow with the portion of dragon's teeth given to Aeetes by Athena from the dragon Cadmus slain at Thebes: "Each of the dragon's teeth will sprout as an armed man, and you are to kill each one as he springs out of the ground." Then Aeetes went away, scoffing at the chances of Jason and his men fulfilling these tasks. Jason went away in despair.

King Aeetes' daughter Medea had overheard all this, and she met Jason that night in the temple of Hecate. She gave him a protective ointment to smear on his body that would protect him from the fire of the brazen bulls; as to the men sprung from the dragon's teeth, she told him of the strategy Cadmus had used—to throw rocks at them and make them so angry that they would fall upon each other in a flurry of sword-strokes and so slay themselves. Jason and Medea began to fall in love.

The golden fleece
THIS 19TH-CENTURY FRENCH ENGRAVING DEPICTS JASON; AFTER EMERGING VICTORIOUS FROM HIS BATTLE WITH THE DRAGON, HE CLAIMS THE GOLDEN FLEECE.

THE GOLDEN FLEECE

Protected by the magic ointment, Jason tamed the bulls and plowed his furrow. Next, he sowed the dragon's teeth in four acres of prepared ground. Night was gathering as the warriors sprouted up, and the plain glittered with their swords, shields, spears, and armor. Jason tossed a stone among them, and it struck the warriors again and again, with the result that they began to fight one another until only a few were left. These Jason slew himself.

Aeetes, enraged, refused to tell Jason where the fleece could be found. During the night, while he plotted further against Jason, Medea stole away to Jason's side and showed him the way to the grove of Ares where the fleece lay hidden, hanging from the branches of a tree and guarded by a dragon. A tumultuous fight ensued. Some say that at one point in the battle, Jason was swallowed by the dragon, only to be vomited up by the spells of Medea, and with the aid of Athena. The dragon was slain; Jason pulled the Golden Fleece from the tree and the two escaped. They made their way back to the Argo and sailed away down the River Phasis. Jason and Medea were married and consummated their union in a sacred cave.

Jason wins the Golden Fleece

THE FLEECE RECOVERED BY JASON WAS THE GOLDEN PELT OF ARIES THE RAM, SACRIFICED TO POSEIDON BY PHRIXUS, HUNG ON A SACRED OAK, AND GUARDED BY A DRAGON. COPPER ENGRAVING (1615–1673)

PLOTS, POTIONS, AND POISON

After many adventures, Jason and Medea arrived home in Greece only to find that Jason's family had all been killed and Pelias was sitting as a tyrant on the throne. Medea deceived the King and his daughters with potions that caused them to believe they saw Artemis flying through the air borne by many dragons; then, by similar arts, she persuaded his daughters to cut Pelias into pieces and boil the pieces in a cauldron. When this deed was discovered, there was a riotous outcry, and Jason and Medea fled aboard the Argo to Corinth.

Jason and Medea

THE DRAGON DEAD AT THEIR FEET, JASON AND MEDEA TAKE THE GOLDEN FLEECE IN THIS 1780 PAINTING BY MARTIN JOHANN SCHMIDT.

There they lived for ten years, and Medea bore Jason two sons. When Medea began to show signs of age and her beauty began to fade, Jason left her to marry Glauce, the daughter of Creon, King of Corinth. He then had Medea banished, along with her sons, as a sorceress.

In retaliation, Medea made garments imbued with fierce poison and placed them in a decorative chest as a wedding gift for Glauce. Medea's two young sons bore the chest to Glauce. They delivered the chest and then returned to their mother's house, where she killed them. When Glauce put on the wedding gifts, they began to burn her to death. Creon rushed to help her, and when he embraced her the flaming robe clung to him also, and both he and Glauce died a horrible death. Jason withdrew to the sea-coast grieving over these events, and when he sat on the shore in the shadow of the Argo, its hull—rotten from years of disuse—collapsed on him and killed him.

SOURCES: THE CADMUS STORY IS RECOUNTED IN *The Library of Apollodorus*, IN HYGINUS'S *Fabulae*, AND IN OVID'S *Metamorphoses*. THE RETELLING GIVEN HERE IS BASED UPON MODERN TRANSLATIONS OF THESE WORKS IN THE LOEB CLASSICAL LIBRARY, WITH ADDITIONAL MATERIAL DRAWN FROM H.J. ROSE, *A Handbook of Greek Mythology* (1958); RICHMOND Y. HATHORN, *Greek Mythology* (1977); JOSEPH FONTENROSE, *Python* (1959); M.P. NILSSON, *The Mycenaean Origins of Greek Mythology* (1972). THE STORY OF JASON ALSO APPEARS IN *Apollodorus* AND *Hyginus*, AND IS RETOLD HERE FROM THESE AND THE OTHER SOURCES CITED ABOVE.

JASON AND THE DRAGON

The earliest Greek poetry only implies that Medea helped Jason to kill the dragon and take the fleece, while Pindar just says that Jason overcame it "by devices." One artefact shows the dragon swallowing Jason then disgorging him; in another, he steals the prize without killing the dragon. Euripides claims Medea killed it, while in Apollonius's *Argonautica*, she merely puts it to sleep.

✦

Herakles

KNOWN IN THE ROMAN WORLD AS HERCULES, HERAKLES IS BEST KNOWN TO MODERN READERS FOR THE "TWELVE LABORS" HE PERFORMED AT THE COMMAND OF EURYSTHEUS. HERAKLES'S ORIGINS AS THE OFFSPRING OF A HUMAN AND A GOD MADE IT UNCLEAR WHETHER HE WAS DIVINE OR NOT, BUT HIS SUPERHUMAN FEATS WERE SUFFICIENT TO GUARANTEE HIM A PLACE IN THE OLYMPIAN PANTHEON. ALL OF HERAKLES'S FEATS INVOLVE A MYTHICAL OR MAGICAL ANIMAL, AND THREE OF THESE ARE DRAGONS OR DRAGONLIKE CREATURES—A CHARACTERISTIC THAT SEEMS TO BE ANTICIPATED IN HIS FIRST ADVENTURE. WHILE STILL A NEWBORN INFANT, HE IS SAID TO HAVE STRANGLED TWO SERPENTS PUT IN THE CRADLE TO KILL HIM AND HIS TWIN BROTHER.

TRAGEDY AND TRICKERY

Alkmene, daughter of the Mycenaean king Elektryon, was the wife of Amphitryon, who received kingship of Mycenae from her father. Shortly after their marriage, Amphitryon was herding Elektryon's cattle. A cow became unruly, and Amphitryon threw a club. It ricocheted off the animal's horns and struck his father-in-law, killing him. In grief, Amphitryon fled into exile in Thebes, whereupon—to win back Alkmene's love—he embarked upon a long war of vengeance against her father's enemies.

Alkmene was beautiful, and in her husband's absence she attracted the admiration of Zeus. On the night he was to complete his journey home, Zeus magically made Amphitryon's road to Thebes three times its normal length. Taking advantage of the delay, Zeus took on the physical form of Amphitryon, went to Alkmene's bed, and slept with her. Later that night, the true Amphitryon arrived home; he, too, went to bed with his wife. Alkmene was later found to be pregnant.

On the day Alkmene was to give birth, and in vengeance for his sleeping with Alkmene, Zeus's wife Hera tricked him into swearing a foolish oath of blessing on any human child born of his bloodline. Hera brought it about so that Alkmene's labor was prolonged, while Menippe—whose husband was descended from Zeus through Perseus—gave birth prematurely: her son Eurystheus thus gained the blessing of Zeus

Master of serpents

HERAKLES WAS DISTINGUISHED FROM EARLIEST YOUTH BY HIS MASTERY OF SERPENTS. THIS 2ND-CENTURY MARBLE SCULPTURE, NOW IN THE CAPITOLINE MUSEUM IN ROME, SHOWS HERAKLES AS A BOY STRANGLING A SNAKE.

NO ORDINARY CHILD

Alkmene finally gave birth. She had not one but two children: twin sons. One of them she named Iphikles; he was the son of Amphitryon and appeared to be a normal child. However, the other twin, named after his paternal grandfather Alkeides, was the offspring of Alkmene's union with Zeus. It was evident immediately that Alkeides was no ordinary child, and that he was destined for great things.

Still jealous over her husband's tryst with Alkmene, Hera sent two poisonous serpents into the twin brothers' cradle to kill them. But Hera's plot was foiled when the infant Alkeides caught and strangled the two serpents—a portent of the great things Alkeides would accomplish.

Under several skillful tutors, Alkeides learned music, wrestling, fencing, and other sports, and by the time he was eighteen he had grown to the height of six feet. He was also very handsome. As a reward for his excellence in sport, Alkeides was invited to a feast at Thespiai by Thespios, who had fifty daughters. While there, Alkeides enjoyed the favors of one of the daughters every night for each of the fifty nights he stayed there, and each one of them bore a son; the oldest and the youngest girls bore twins. On his return to Thebes, Alkeides earned King Kreon's favor by defeating King Erginos, an enemy of the Thebans. As a reward, Alkeides received Kreon's daughter Megara in marriage.

THE TWELVE LABORS OF HERAKLES

For many years, their marriage was a happy one, and Megara bore Alkeides several children. But Hera, still seething, caused Alkeides to experience fits of insane violence. In one of these, Alkeides fell into false suspicion of his wife and children, and he slew his whole family. Coming to himself again, Alkeides left Thebes in exile. Seeking advice from the Oracle, he went to Delphi, where the prophetess renamed him Herakles, "the glory of Hera." She also condemned him to serve Menippe's son King Eurystheus, who had usurped the blessing of Zeus at his birth years earlier. If Herakles could serve Eurystheus faithfully for twelve years, he would be rewarded with immortality.

Now Herakles met and fell in love with Deïaneira; in order to win her hand, he was required to fight Acheloos, a river-god. Acheloos was able to transform his shape, and during their struggle, he assumed the form of an enormous water-monster. But Herakles had encountered serpents before, and though this one was larger, Herakles was now much stronger. He grappled with the monster and mastered him, and he and Deïaneira were wed. They remained married for many years, and she bore him a son and a daughter.

Moved either by the Fates or by his own ill-will, Eurystheus demanded that Herakles perform twelve glorious deeds—seemingly impossible tasks—none of which did he expect him to complete. But Herakles succeeded: he killed and skinned the invulnerable Nemean lion, taking

***Herakles and the Hydra,
Antonio Pollaiolo (1432–1498)***
HERAKLES USES VARIOUS WEAPONS IN DIFFERENT DEPICTIONS OF HIS FIGHT WITH THE HYDRA. HERE HE CLUBS THE MONSTER SENSELESS BEFORE CUTTING OFF ITS HEADS.

DRAGON GUARDIANS

GREEK MYTHOLOGY IS TEEMING WITH DRAGONS AND MONSTROUS SERPENTS OF ALL DESCRIPTIONS. THE GREEK WORD FOR "DRAGON" MEANT "THE SHARP-SIGHTED," OR "CREATURE WITH FLASHING EYES." FROM THIS SYMBOLIC NAMING CAME THE DRAGON'S ROLE AS A GUARDIAN OF PRECIOUS OBJECTS— FOR EXAMPLE, SACRED SPRINGS, THE GOLDEN FLEECE, AND THE GOLDEN APPLES OF THE HESPERIDES.

✦

its pelt as his cloak. He captured four uncatchable beasts: the Erymanthian Boar, the Golden Hind of Keryneia, the Cretan Bull, and Cerberus, the Hound of Hades; he tamed the horses of Diomedes, who fed on human flesh; he drove away the man-eating Symphalian Birds with arrow-sharp feathers; he diverted the river Alpheios through the stables of Augeias, cleansing it in one day of centuries of accumulated filth. He defeated the Amazons, taking the precious girdle of their queen, Hippolyte. And, in further fulfilment of the portent whereby he slew the serpents in his cradle, Herakles faced three monstrous dragons.

THE HYDRA

In the swamps of Lerna there lived an enormous serpent—the many-headed Hydra, offspring of Typhon and Echidna. This monster ravaged the countryside, killing both cattle and people. It was originally furnished with nine heads, one of them immortal. It was a special property of the monster that when one of its mortal heads was cut off, two grew in its place; by the time Herakles went to battle against it, its heads numbered a hundred or more. Herakles mounted a chariot driven by Iolaos and rode to Lerna, where he found the creature beside a spring near its den on the side of a hill. Herakles had the assistance of Iolaos, who brought flaming brands to the scene: whenever Herakles cut off one of the Hydra's heads, Iolaos cauterized the headless stump with fire, thus preventing its regrowth.

One by one, Herakles thus succeeded in cutting off all the monster's heads, until only the immortal head was left. This too he sliced off with one mighty stroke of his sword. The headless Hydra lay dead in a pool of its own poisonous blood. Herakles dipped the tips of his arrows in the blood, ensuring the quick death of anyone wounded by one of his arrows thereafter.

GERYON

In the far west of the world lay the sunset-red island of Erytheie, on which lived a herd of cattle. They were tended by Eurytion and guarded by a Geryon, an enormous dragon. The task of Herakles was to find the island, kill the dragon, capture the herd of cattle, and bring them home.

Herakles made the long journey to the island. Upon arrival, he killed Eurytion along with his dog Orthos. Then he faced Geryon, who had a human face, scales and coils ending in a spiked tail, and a spiked spine. Using up half his poisoned arrows, Herakles managed to slay Geryon.

A seven-headed Hydra
THE HYDRA'S HEADS DIFFER IN NUMBER IN VARIOUS ANCIENT GREEK TEXTS, FROM AS FEW AS FIVE TO AS MANY AS A HUNDRED. EVENTUALLY THE FIGURE BECAME STANDARDIZED AS NINE.

Dante's Inferno

DANTE BORROWED MONSTERS FROM GREEK MYTHOLOGY IN *THE INFERNO*. IN THIS MANUSCRIPT ILLUSTRATION FROM THE VATICAN LIBRARY (c. 313 ce), DANTE AND VIRGIL RIDE ON GERYON'S BACK INTO THE CIRCLE OF THE FRAUDULENTS.

His journey home with the Erytheian cattle was long and arduous. Near the Black Sea, he was beguiled by a monstrous woman in serpentine form; in Sicily, he wrestled and killed King Eryx; but eventually he reached Thebes and presented the cattle of Erytheie to Eurystheus.

LADON

The greatest challenge was yet to come. Eurystheus charged Herakles with the task of journeying west once again—this time to Arcadia, to the fabulous garden of the Hesperides. There, in the center of the garden, grew a marvelous tree given to Hera upon her marriage to Zeus. The fruits of this tree were golden apples, which, it was said, granted immortality. The tree was tended by the three Hesperides—Aigle, Erytheia, and Arethusa—the daughters of Night; it was guarded by the dragon Ladon. Herakles's task was to pluck the golden apples and bring them to Eurystheus. Herakles made his journey, which was even more arduous than the previous one. When he arrived in Arcadia he found that the entrance to the garden was a closely guarded secret. Nereus, a god of the sea, divulged the secret way into the garden, and Herakles found a watchful dragon guarding the path to the marvelous tree. By some means which is not known, he charmed the dragon so that it fell asleep, and once it was asleep, Herakles slew it and took the apples.

Herakles had many other adventures, and some of these included battles against other dragons or monstrous serpents. In one of these, he fought and slew the sea-monster called Triton. In another, he rescued Troy and its king Laomedon from a huge sea monster sent by Poseidon. The monster swallowed Herakles whole, and Herakles cut his way out from the dragon's belly, which led to its death.

SOURCES: JAMES G. FRAZER, ED. AND TRANS., APOLLODORUS: *THE LIBRARY* (1921); RICHMOND Y. HATHORN, *GREEK MYTHOLOGY* (1977); H.J. ROSE, *A HANDBOOK OF GREEK MYTHOLOGY* (1928); H.G. EVELYN-WHITE, TRANS., HESIOD, *HOMERIC HYMNS, EPIC CYCLE, HOMERICA* (1914).

St. Michael

THE MYTH OF MICHAEL THE ARCHANGEL SLAYING THE DRAGON IS BASED UPON THE BIBLICAL *BOOK OF REVELATION* BY ST. JOHN. THE BOOK READS: "NOW WAR AROSE IN HEAVEN, MICHAEL AND HIS ANGELS FIGHTING AGAINST THE DRAGON; AND THE DRAGON AND HIS ANGELS FOUGHT, BUT THEY WERE DEFEATED AND THERE WAS NO LONGER ANY PLACE FOR THEM IN HEAVEN. AND THE GREAT DRAGON WAS CAST OUT, THAT ANCIENT SERPENT, WHO IS CALLED THE DEVIL AND SATAN, THE DECEIVER OF THE WHOLE WORLD—HE WAS THROWN DOWN TO THE EARTH, AND HIS ANGELS WERE THROWN DOWN WITH HIM." *(REV. 12:7–9)*

THE SERPENT'S REVENGE

The text goes on to describe this as a spiritual victory equal to salvation and the coming of God's kingdom. But further on, we learn that though the dragon has been cast down, it has not yet been destroyed:

AND WHEN THE DRAGON SAW THAT HE HAD BEEN THROWN DOWN TO THE EARTH, HE PURSUED THE WOMAN WHO HAD BORNE THE MALE CHILD. BUT THE WOMAN WAS GIVEN THE TWO WINGS OF THE GREAT EAGLE THAT SHE MIGHT FLY FROM THE SERPENT INTO THE WILDERNESS, TO THE PLACE WHERE SHE IS TO BE NOURISHED FOR A TIME, AND TIMES, AND HALF A TIME. THE SERPENT POURED WATER LIKE A RIVER OUT OF HIS MOUTH AFTER THE WOMAN, TO SWEEP HER AWAY WITH THE FLOOD. BUT THE EARTH CAME TO THE HELP OF THE WOMAN, AND THE EARTH OPENED ITS MOUTH AND SWALLOWED THE RIVER WHICH THE DRAGON HAD POURED FROM HIS MOUTH.

St. Michael and angels

IN THIS FRENCH 14TH-CENTURY TAPESTRY, ST. MICHAEL AND HIS ANGELS FIGHT THE DRAGON. IN THE BIBLE, ST. MICHAEL IS THE EQUIVALENT OF ST. GEORGE. AROUND EUROPE, THERE ARE CHURCHES DEDICATED TO THE SAINT ON MOUNTAINTOPS, WHICH ARE BELIEVED TO BE THE HOME OF DRAGONS.

Men worship beast

IN THIS ILLUSTRATION FROM REVELATIONS CHAPTER 13 IN THE BIBLE, A MANY-HEADED DRAGON EMERGES FROM THE SEA, OFFERS HIS POWER TO A BEAST, AND IS WORSHIPPED BY ALL MEN.

THEN THE DRAGON WAS ANGRY WITH THE WOMAN, AND WENT OFF TO MAKE WAR ON THE REST OF HER OFFSPRING, ON THOSE WHO KEEP THE COMMANDMENTS OF GOD AND BEAR TESTIMONY TO JESUS. AND THEN I STOOD ON THE SAND OF THE SEA. (REV. 12:13—17)

The ten-headed beast St. John later describes rising out of the sea is often interpreted in art and biblical commentary as a kind of dragon, particularly because "to it the dragon gave his power and his throne and great authority" *(Rev. 13:2)*. Not until near the end of the *Book of Revelation* is the dragon finally caught, chained, and imprisoned:

THEN I SAW AN ANGEL COMING DOWN FROM HEAVEN, HOLDING IN HIS HAND THE KEY OF THE BOTTOMLESS PIT AND A GREAT CHAIN. AND HE SEIZED THE DRAGON, THAT ANCIENT SERPENT, WHO IS THE DEVIL AND SATAN, AND BOUND HIM FOR A THOUSAND YEARS, AND THREW HIM INTO THE PIT, AND SHUT IT AND SEALED IT OVER HIM, THAT HE SHOULD DECEIVE THE NATIONS NO MORE, TILL THE THOUSAND YEARS WERE ENDED. AFTER THAT HE MUST BE LOOSED FOR A LITTLE WHILE AND WHEN THE THOUSAND YEARS ARE ENDED,

SATAN WILL BE LOOSED FROM HIS PRISON AND WILL COME OUT TO DECEIVE THE NATIONS WHICH ARE AT THE FOUR CORNERS OF THE EARTH, THAT IS, GOG AND MAGOG, TO GATHER THEM FOR BATTLE; THEIR NUMBER IS LIKE THE SAND OF THE SEA. AND THEY MARCHED UP OVER THE BROAD EARTH AND SURROUNDED THE CAMP OF THE SAINTS AND THE BELOVED CITY; BUT FIRE CAME DOWN FROM HEAVEN AND CONSUMED THEM, AND THE DEVIL WHO HAD DECEIVED THEM WAS THROWN INTO THE LAKE OF FIRE AND SULPHUR WHERE THE BEAST AND THE FALSE PROPHET WERE, AND THEY WILL BE TORMENTED DAY AND NIGHT FOR EVER AND EVER. (REV. 20:1–3, 7–10)

The angel holding the key and the chain at the beginning of this passage is assumed by most commentators to be St. Michael.

THE SAINT IN COMBAT

The cult of St. Michael was very popular in the early Middle Ages, and St. Michael has often been regarded as the patron of St. George, also a dragon-slayer. Many churches, towns, and villages throughout Europe are named after St. Michael. Of particular note is St. Michael's Mount, a tidal island off the coast of Penwith in Cornwall, England. In keeping with the mysterious or spiritual qualities associated with such places, the island has a 15th-century chapel. Mont Saint-Michel off the coast of Normandy has a Benedictine abbey dating from the eighth century.

St. Michael and the Dragon of the Apocalypse are popular subjects in religious art. Innumerable icons and paintings in the Orthodox and Catholic traditions show the saint in combat with the apocalyptic dragon; Renaissance painters including Tintoretto, Raphael, and Carapaccio explored the subject. Albrecht Dürer's 1498 woodcut showing the winged archangel spearing the dragon in the sky is particularly stirring.

St. Michael slaying the dragon
ACCORDING TO LEGEND, ST. MICHAEL APPEARED IN NUMEROUS LOCATIONS IN BRITAIN AND EUROPE DURING THE 4TH AND 5TH CENTURIES; IT IS SAID THAT IN MANY PLACES HE SLEW DRAGONS.

Perseus and Andromeda

THE MYTH OF PERSEUS'S FIGHT AGAINST THE DRAGON OF SERIPHOS IS JUSTLY REGARDED AS HIS MOST FAMOUS VENTURE, BUT HIS ENCOUNTER WITH THE GORGONS AND THE DECAPITATION OF SERPENT-HAIRED MEDUSA IS ALMOST AS POPULAR, IN ART, LITERATURE, AND SAINTS' LEGENDS. THE INFLUENCE OF THE STORY ON THE LEGEND OF ST. GEORGE IS OBVIOUS AND OVERWHELMING—FOR ALL PRACTICAL PURPOSES, THE STORY OF ST. GEORGE AND THE DRAGON IS A THINLY VEILED RETELLING OF THE PERSEUS LEGEND. SIMILARITIES BETWEEN THIS MYTH AND THE ANCIENT NEAR EASTERN MYTHS OF GODS SLAYING DRAGONS OF THE SEA ARE JUST AS OBVIOUS, AND NO DOUBT IT IS THESE ECHOES THAT MADE THE MYTH SO COMPELLING A PATTERN FOR NUMEROUS LATER RETELLINGS.

GOLDEN RAIN

Acrisius, king of Argos, had been told by the Oracle at Delphi that he would be killed by the son of Danae, his daughter. In an effort to keep his daughter from bearing children, Acrisius had Danae imprisoned in a bronze tower without doors, thus preventing men from having access to her. The roof of the tower was open to the heavens, however, and Zeus—who sees all things from on high—saw the beauty of Danae as she bathed in the sun, and he desired her.

Perseus rescuing Andromeda, 1602

IN THIS OIL ON CANVAS BY GIUSEPPE CESARI,
PERSEUS RIDES IN ON HIS CHARGER TO RESCUE
ANDROMEDA. NAKED AND CHAINED TO A
ROCK, SHE HAD BEEN LEFT AT THE MERCY OF
A FEROCIOUS DRAGON.

Taking the form of a golden rain, Zeus descended upon Danae in a flood of ecstasy that left her expecting a child. In the course of time, she gave birth to a son. She named him Perseus.

When he discovered he had been betrayed, Acrisius seized Danae and her infant son, locked them in a wooden chest and set it adrift on the Aegean Sea, which was wracked by storms. But Zeus was unwilling to let his son die in this way, and he went to Poseidon, the lord of the waves, entreating him to calm the sea, and thus save mother and son from certain death. The sea grew calm, but not before the chest was buffeted so severely that the lock was broken and the lid loosened. Then, on a calm ocean breeze Danae and Perseus were blown to the island of Seriphos.

THE GORGONS

There was a fisherman on Seriphos by the name of Dictys, whose brother Polydectes was king of the island, and he and his wife took the two in, providing them with food and shelter, saving them from starvation. There they stayed for many years. Perseus grew older and stronger, becoming in time a handsome young man.

When King Polydectes saw the beautiful Danae, he desired her but feared her son Perseus would prevent him from wooing her or taking her by force; so he made a plan. Polydectes ordered Perseus to go in search of the Gorgons, three monstrous sisters, and not to return until he had slain Medusa and severed her head. He must bring the head back in proof that he had accomplished this quest. But Polydectes did not reveal to Perseus that anyone who looked Medusa in the eye would be turned to stone.

Athena came to Perseus and told him of the dangers awaiting him, and gave him a polished shield, instructing him not to look directly at Medusa but to look at her reflection in the mirror-like shield. In this way, she said, he would avoid the curse. Hermes came to him and give him winged sandals with which to escape by magic. When at last he discovered the Gorgons, Perseus approached Medusa by walking backward and keeping his gaze focused on her reflection in the shield. Then he drew his unbreakable sword and cut off her head, and shoved it in a sack. Before the other monstrous women could overtake him, Perseus flew away on the winged sandals.

PERSEUS AND ANDROMEDA

On his return journey to Seriphos, Perseus found a young woman chained to a cliff by the sea. When he asked why this was so, the people of that country told him Poseidon had punished the maiden, Andromeda, in this way because her mother, Cassiopeia, had said she was more beautiful than the Nereids, Poseidon's daughters. However, the people did not tell Perseus the truth, which was this: in revenge for the insult to his daughters, Poseidon had sent an enormous flood to inundate the coastal cities, and he had sent a dragon to capture and devour the people as they tried to escape. The people had seized Andromeda, dragged her down to the ocean, and chained her to the cliff as a sacrifice, hoping to soothe the dragon and appease the angry Poseidon.

Perseus went to Cephus, Andromeda's father, and offered to slay the dragon and set Andromeda free; in this way he wished to win her hand in marriage. This was agreed. And so Perseus returned to the seaside

The Gorgon's head
AN EARLY 20TH-CENTURY ILLUSTRATION OF
PERSEUS SHOWING THE GORGON'S HEAD,
WHICH TURNED HIS ATTACKERS TO STONE.

where Andromeda was hanging from the cliff by unbreakable iron chains. Soon there was an enormous roar from far out in the ocean, and a dragon appeared. It made its way to land, its gigantic jaw opened wide; steam and hot breath hissed from its mouth and nostrils. First Perseus threw stones at it, but to no avail. The dragon advanced and, as Andromeda looked on, helpless, it trapped Perseus between its enormous jaws and swallowed him whole. Within the beast's hideous belly, Perseus drew his adamantine sword—diamond-edged—and cut his way out, killing it from the inside out. Then with mighty strokes he cut off the monster's head. He went to Andromeda and, using his sword of adamant, he cut the iron chains binding her to the rocky cliff face. He took the frightened maiden home to her father. When Cephus saw with his own eyes that his daughter had been freed, Perseus reminded him of their agreement.

TURNED TO STONE

Not long afterward the wedding feast was held, but in the middle of the feast, Andromeda's father Cephus had a change of heart. He began to back down from his offer, saying Andromeda had been promised in marriage earlier to Phineas, and only the trouble with Poseidon had prevented the union from going forward. Perseus protested, whereupon Phineas and his men attacked him, hoping to slay him. But Perseus pulled the head of Medusa from the bag in which he had concealed it, and when they looked into her eyes, they were all turned to stone.

At last Perseus returned to Seriphos with Andromeda, only to find that Polydectes had intensified his efforts to win his mother Danae, resorting to force. He had seized his brother Dictys and put him in prison. Danae

Saints and Dragons

Many saints in the Christian tradition are credited with the taming or slaying of dragons. The idea originates in biblical passages describing Yahweh's power over sea-monsters (e.g., Job 41; Ps. 74:13–14; Ps. 91:13), the gospel passage granting Jesus' disciples power over serpents (Mk 16:18), and the account of St. Michael the archangel's victory over Satan, the dragon of the apocalypse (Rev. 12:3–9; 20:1–3). The prototype for the sacred biography of holy men and women is the early life of St. Anthony, which describes demons attacking Anthony in the form of unspecified "wild beasts" whose teeth, horns, and claws tear his flesh.

St. Silvester of Rome is said to have bound the jaws of a dragon kept in a pit beneath the city, saving the Roman people from its deadly breath.

"fear not, dear maiden, but be glad: for this most ferocious enemy has been defeated by the power of god and henceforward will do you no harm."

Full chivalric splendor

Clad in full armor, equipped with a lance, and mounted on a white charger, St. George advances in full chivalric splendor to rescue the virginal princess of Silena. Paolo Ucello's painting of the scene (c. 1455–1460) evokes some of the subtle eroticism latent in the story.

HOLY POWER

St. George leapt upon his horse even as the dragon came crawling out of the water toward the maiden. He made the sign of the cross, set his lance beneath his right arm, and sprang toward the dragon. Galloping at full speed, he thrust the lance into the dragon's open mouth and down its throat so that the dragon was pinned to the earth. It lay upon the beach as if dead.

George said to the maiden, "Fear not, dear maiden, but be glad: for this most ferocious enemy has been defeated by the power of God and henceforward will do you no harm."

"Now," he said, "take your sash and bind it fast around the dragon's neck." She answered, "I dare not go so close to it." The knight replied, "Good maiden, do as I have said and it will not harm you, for the Lord God is going to work a great miracle both for your sake and that of the people of your city."

She went to the dragon, loosened her sash, and bound the dragon with it. God rewarded this gesture, for the monster became as gentle as a lamb. Then St. George said, "Go back home into the city, leading the dragon along behind you." This she did, and the dragon came along behind as if it were a tamed little lap-dog on its master's leash.

THE ONE TRUE GOD

When she came into the city, the people began to cry out, saying, "Flee! Flee the fiend lest it kill us all!" George bade them not to flee, telling them it would do them no harm if they would heed his command. The king rejoiced to see his daughter alive and then greeted St. George, asking what his errand there might be. George said he had been sent to free the maiden and save the city, but they must now agree to abandon the worship of false idols and believe in the one true God who had made heaven and earth and all things in it.

"If you do as I have said, I will slay the dragon. But if you do not, I will let it loose again to work what havoc it wishes." They all shouted out with one voice: "Valiant warrior, do not let the dragon loose: we will gladly do as you command." With that, St. George hewed off the dragon's head and ordered its lifeless body to be dragged out of the city. Four teams of donkeys and oxen were required, owing to the dragon's monstrous size. Twenty thousand people received baptism on that day; the king had a church built in honor of the blessed Virgin Mary and St. George, and a spring flowed from beneath the altar of the church whose sweet waters cured all sickness and infirmity.

SOURCES: THIS ADAPTATION IS BASED ON THE MEDIEVAL LATIN "LIFE OF ST. GEORGE" FOUND IN *THE GOLDEN LEGEND* BY JACOBUS DE VORAGINE AND THE SANCTUARIUM OF BONINUS MOMBRITIUS; ON AN ADAPTATION OF THE SAINT'S LIFE IN THE LATE MEDIEVAL ICELANDIC *REYKJAHÓLABÓK*; AND ON THE MODERN TRANSLATION OF *THE GOLDEN LEGEND*, WILLIAM GRANGER RYAN'S *JACOBUS DE VORAGINE: THE GOLDEN LEGEND* (2 VOLS., 1993).

St. Samson
and the
Dragons
of Dol
and Pental

St. Samson was a bishop in South Wales *circa* 490 CE, and he died at the monastery at Dol in Brittany, which he founded, *circa* 565 CE. His feastday is July 28. His biography, called "A Vita" in Latin, is the earliest recorded life of a saint in the British Celtic church. St. Samson's four encounters with dragons are all similar in their general details: in his missionary travels, people tell him of ferocious dragons devastating their lands; the saint approaches the monster and, through the power of God, first tames the dragon, then kills it. Three of the four episodes from the life of St. Samson probably originated in the text of the first version of the saint's vita, written in the early 7th century; the fourth one, however, seems to be a later addition to the legend. Translated adaptations of the first and the fourth are given here.

. . . .

A DRAGON IN THE FOREST

Together with his father, Ammon, his uncle, and their deacon, Samson was traveling back to his monastery, teaching and preaching to his companions concerning the parables of the Old and New Testaments. Along the way, Ammon saw a footpath leading into the forest, and it looked as if the ground all around had been burned. It appeared also that a beam had been dragged across the weeds, which were also burned.

Troubled by the sight of these things, Ammon first showed the track to his brother and said, "The dragon we heard about in our parents' house must be in this very forest, and not very far ahead of us." Samson understood well enough what they were saying to one another; nevertheless, he asked, "Father, what are you two discussing?" Ammon replied, "I see that a dragon has gone ahead of us."

TAMING THE SERPENT

With a quiet spirit, Samson consoled them and, telling them not to be afraid, he calmly quoted to them the scripture in which Our Lord said, "If you had faith as a grain of mustard, you would say unto this mountain, 'Be thou removed from here,' and it would go; for nothing shall be impossible unto you." "Therefore," said Samson, "remain steadfast, trust in God, and wait until I return to you victorious. But no matter what you may hear, remain silent." Even as he was leaving them, however, his uncle began following him, saying it was not right that he should go into such danger alone and asking to go with him. But Samson replied that since God was with him, he was not alone, and he repeated his instruction that they should wait there until he returned.

Striding away quickly through the burned underbrush, he saw in the distance the head of a fiery serpent crawling along in the middle of a wide area of devastation. Seeing the dragon, Samson lifted up his voice and said loudly: "The Lord is my light and my salvation; of whom then

DIVINE POWER

THE DRAGON IS A BIBLICAL SYMBOL OF SATANIC EVIL; MOST MEDIEVAL SAINTS— UNTIL ST. GEORGE— WERE NOT MILITARY FIGURES BUT AGENTS OF PEACE AND SALVATION. ST. SAMSON QUELLS THE DRAGON BY MAKING THE SIGN OF THE CROSS, GIRDLING ITS NECK WITH HIS CINCTURE, AND PRONOUNCING ITS DEATH. MOST BRITISH SAINTS DO NOT FIGHT THE MONSTER PHYSICALLY BUT RELY ON DIVINE POWER TO VANQUISH THE DEMONIC ENEMY.

✠

should I be afraid?" Hearing Samson's voice and detecting the scent of the saint, the serpent angrily twisted its head around toward its tail; but Samson ran towards the serpent just as if he had seen a tiny snake. Seeing this, the serpent roared as if it had been stabbed with a sword, coiled itself into a circle, and with its teeth bit down upon its own tail.

Signing himself with the cross, St. Samson said, "Bless the Lord, all ye works of the Lord; praise and exalt him above all things forever." Having said this, he called to his comrades, saying, "Come and see the work of the Lord, who is more fearsome than anything inhabiting the earth, that your faith may be firmly established." When they drew near, they saw the serpent rolling around in a circle, unable to lift up its head at all. Then Samson said to the serpent, "May you live no more," and immediately the serpent lifted up its head and stood up on its tail, forming itself into a ridiculous-looking circle. It vomited out all its poison and died most horribly.

THE MONASTERY AT PENTAL

Near the end of his life, before he entered the monastery at Dol which he had founded many years before, St. Samson stayed in a monastery at Pental. Now old and infirm, he made his retreat there for both physical and spiritual rest. On a certain occasion, the brothers brought him reports concerning a dragon that was doing harm to the region nearby. This dragon was more dangerous than any he had dealt with before. With the saintly compassion which was customary to him, Samson— accompanied by a number of the brothers—made the arduous journey up the mountain to where the dragon's lair was suspected to be.

When he saw smoke mixed with fire rising from the mountain, he said to the brothers, "Behold the place of the dragon!" Trembling with fear, they replied, "Father, people are not accustomed to venture into this place. Perhaps if we go away and leave the dragon alone it will not wreak any further destruction. Besides, you are old and ill. Let us depart." But St. Samson replied, "Although I may be ill, I have the power of the eternal, invincible God on my side. Stay here if you wish," he said, "but I will go to face the monster. Go to the top of the mountain and wait for me there."

THE SWORD OF THE SPIRIT

Armed with the shield of faith, the sword of the Spirit, and the breastplate of hope, Samson continued on to the dragon's cave. He stood before it and ordered it to come out. When the dragon heard his voice, it emerged, trembling with fear. Samson put his stole around its neck and dragged it up the mountain. They approached the summit, where the brothers were waiting the outcome of Samson's encounter with the fiend. When they caught sight of the dragon, they became terrified and started to flee. But Samson said they should fear the God who made all things, rather than any creature. Then, in front of them all, Samson commanded the dragon in the name of Christ to take itself to the sea and die. The dragon obeyed, went down to the sea, plunged in, and drowned. The brothers all returned to Pental with Samson and were united in their praise to God.

SOURCES: BASED UPON THE ORIGINAL LATIN TEXT IN CONJUNCTION WITH LATER TRANSLATIONS IN ENGLISH AND FRENCH: THOMAS TAYLOR, *THE LIFE OF ST. SAMSON OF DOL* (1925); ROBERT FAWTIER, *LA VIE DE SAINT SAMSON; ESSAI DE CRITIQUE HAGIOGRAPHIQUE* (1912); PIERRE FLOBERT, *LA VIE ANCIENNE DE SAINT SAMSON DE DOL* (1997); CHRISTINE RAUER, *BEOWULF AND THE DRAGON: SOURCES AND ANALOGUES* (2000); F. PLAINE, "VITA ANTIQUA SANCTI SAMSONIS DOLENSIS EPISCOPI," *ANALECTA BOLLANDIANA* I (1882): 209–58; F. PLAINE, *LA TRÈS ANCIENNE VIE INEDITE DE ST. SAMSON* (1887).

FIREY DARTS

ST. SAMSON'S DEFENSIVE ARMOR IS BASED LOOSELY ON A PAULINE ALLEGORY IN EPHESIANS 6:10-17. THERE, THE SERVANTS OF GOD CONTEND AGAINST SATANIC EVIL, EQUIPPED WITH THE BELT OF TRUTH, THE BREASTPLATE OF RIGHTEOUSNESS, THE SHOES OF PEACE, AND THE SHIELD OF FAITH. THE SHIELD IS USED TO QUENCH THE "FIERY DARTS OF THE EVIL ONE."

✢

Sigurd and Fáfnir

THE STORY OF THE ENCOUNTER BETWEEN THE SCANDINAVIAN HERO SIGURD AND THE MONSTROUS DRAGON NAMED FÁFNIR IS TOLD IN FIVE MAIN VERSIONS SURVIVING IN OLD ICELANDIC MANUSCRIPTS, AND IS ALLUDED TO IN MANY SHORT POEMS IN THE OLD NORSE TRADITION. THE STORY IS ALSO DEPICTED IN ROCK CARVINGS AND OTHER FORMS OF ARCHEOLOGY SURVIVING FROM THE EARLY MIDDLE AGES. THE IMAGE MOST OFTEN DISCOVERED SHOWS THE MOMENT WHEN SIGURD STABS FÁFNIR FROM BENEATH, BUT MANY CARVINGS ALSO DEPICT THE FORGING OF SIGURD'S SWORD, THE ROASTING OF FÁFNIR'S HEART ON A SPIT, AND SIGURD'S HORSE GRANI LOADED WITH TREASURE FROM THE DRAGON'S HOARD. SIGURD WAS REGARDED AS THE MOST FAMOUS DRAGONSLAYER IN THE GERMANIC MYTHIC TRADITION: BEFORE HIS BIRTH, SIGURD'S FATHER PROPHESIED THAT, "HIS NAME WILL BE RENOWNED AS LONG AS THE WORLD LASTS."

THE SAGA OF THE VÖLSUNGS

The version of the story given here is based upon the highly accessible prose narrative called *The Saga of the Völsungs*, with additional details drawn from the *Poetic Edda*, a 13th-century compendium that gives the most complete picture of pre-Christian Scandinavian mythology.

The idea that a human being could be transformed into a dragon is among the most interesting features of the Scandinavian dragon myth seen in this story, which also corroborates the early Germanic mythic conception of the dragon as a ferocious hoarder of treasure. The dragon's greedy nature has been seen as a symbolic expression of instability in the human social world caused by greed. Successful warriors and powerful rulers are shown again and again in medieval culture to be particularly susceptible to the twin temptations of pride and greed; two cardinal sins in the medieval religious tradition that produce metaphorical—if not real—monstrous transformations in people who give in to them.

ODIN AND THE SWORD

Sigurd was the son of Sigmund, whose father Völsung was one of the most powerful kings in Hunaland and a descendent of Odin. The warriors in the line of Völsung were renowned in the north for their prowess and victory in battle, and Sigurd was the greatest among them.

Sigurd was sprung from nobility, and his sword, named Gram, was the gift of a god. In the middle of his grandfather Völsung's royal hall there grew an enormous tree named Barnstock, whose roots went deep into the ground and whose branches went through the roof and up toward the open sky. As a test of Völsung's men and as a sign of his favor, Odin appeared one day and plunged a sword into the trunk of Barnstock up to the hilt. Odin said, "Whoever pulls this sword from the tree can have it as my gift. He who has it will know that he never owned a better sword." Now Völsung had ten sons, and after the strongest warriors in the kingdom and Völsung's other sons had tried without success, his

Song of the Nibelungs
Sigurd kills the dragon in this color lithograph by R.E. Kepler, 1890.

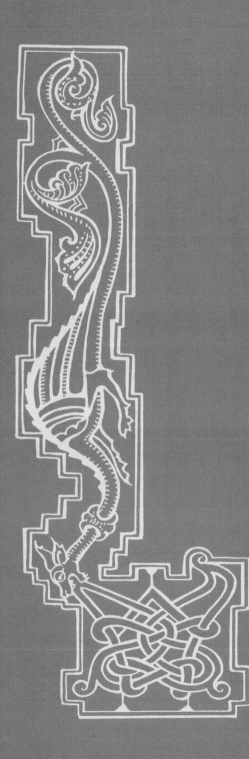

youngest son Sigmund pulled it easily from the tree. A rival king, Siggeir, who was present in Völsung's hall to witness this feat, asked to buy the sword. But Sigmund refused.

Siggeir took revenge by attacking and slaying Völsung and all his sons. Only Sigmund escaped by means of his wondrous sword, and he vowed revenge. With his son Sinfjotli, Sigmund went on many expeditions, and their prowess as hunters and warriors grew. Finally, remembering his vow, Sigmund stole into King Siggeir's hall with Sinfjotli seeking vengeance. They burned the hall to the ground and escaped, using the sword to cut their way free through the solid rock.

SIGMUND AND HJORDIS

Sigmund fell in love with Hjordis, daughter of King Eylimi, but King Lyngvi also desired her. Hjordis chose Sigmund. The nuptials were celebrated with much feasting, and the two returned to rule in Hunaland. Soon jealous King Lyngvi arrived and attacked Sigmund's forces with a vast army. Throughout the battle, Sigmund performed valiantly with the sword he had pulled from Barnstock. But late in the day an old one-eyed man in a black hooded robe and wide-brimmed hat came onto the battlefield armed with a spear. He attacked Sigmund, who struck back with his sword; but it broke in two against the spear and Sigmund was mortally wounded. Night fell, and the battlefield was littered with the dead and dying. Hjordis came through the darkness onto the battlefield and found her husband still alive. Breathing his last, he told her she was expecting a child. "He will be a boy," said the dying king, "and his name will be renowned as long as the world lasts." Then he was dead.

Alf, son of King Hjalprek of Denmark, found Hjordis and took her and the Völsungs' immense wealth to Denmark. Within a few months, Hjordis gave birth to a son; his piercing eyes were noted by King Hjalprek, who called him "Sigurd." As the saga says, "Whenever the renowned kings and nobles of old are named, Sigurd's strength, prowess, vigor, and valor are called foremost among them all." Sigurd was reared in Hjalprek's court and fostered by a metal-smith named Regin, son of Hreidmar.

SIGURD AND REGIN

One day, when the lad was not yet full grown, Regin asked Sigurd about his ancestral wealth. Sigurd replied that it was being watched over by kings, whom he trusted to guard it better than he could. Not long after, Regin asked him again, taunting him for being an orphan and penniless. He continued to goad Sigurd in this manner. "For a young man of royal blood," he said, "you have far too little wealth."

Then he told Sigurd where he could get a great deal of treasure for very little effort. "Not far from here, on Gnita Heath," he said, "someone called Fáfnir has a pile of gold larger than you have ever seen in one place before."

"Yes," said Sigurd, "I've heard of Fáfnir—a dragon so large that no one dares approach him or his gold."

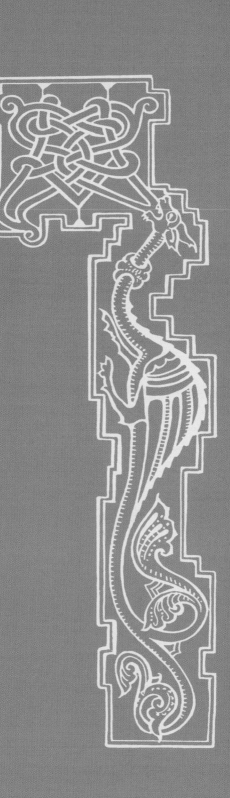

"NOT SO!" REGIN REPLIED. **"ACTUALLY HE'S NO LARGER THAN A GRASS SNAKE, AND SO WOULD YOUR FATHER AND GRANDFATHER HAVE SAID. BUT PERHAPS YOU AREN'T MADE OF THE SAME STOUT STUFF THEY WERE."**

"THAT MAY OR MAY NOT BE THE CASE," SAID SIGURD, **"BUT THERE IS NO REASON TO RIDICULE ME THAT WAY, SINCE I AM SCARCELY PAST MY YOUTH. BUT WHY DO YOU URGE ME TO THIS?"**

"AH, NOW: THERE'S A STORY BEHIND THAT," SAID REGIN.

A dragon in a cave with skulls
SCANDINAVIAN DRAGONS, AS IN THIS 1920 ILLUSTRATION, OFTEN OCCUPY CAVES FILLED WITH HIDDEN TREASURE. THESE MAY EQUATE WITH STONE-AGE PASSAGE-GRAVES AND BURIAL CHAMBERS, WHICH OFTEN HOUSED THE CORPSE AND PRECIOUS POSSESSIONS.

the dwarf's gold

my father was hreidmar, and my brothers were otr and fáfnir. i was the youngest and the least regarded, but i knew how to work iron, silver, gold, and make lots of useful things. otr, a skillful hunter, took the form of an otter by day, and often dove into deep pools and caught fish. fáfnir was big and tough-looking, and he always wanted possession of everything.

there was a pool under a waterfall in which there lived a dwarf named andvari. he often took the form of a pike and there caught his food, for the pool was full of fish. one day, my brother otr caught a salmon. the three gods odin, loki, and hoenir were passing by on a journey just as otr was about to eat the fish. for sport, loki threw a stone and struck and killed otr. the gods skinned otr and took the otter-pelt and went on their way. that night they came to my father's house and showed us the pelt. we made them our captives, and, as ransom, demanded that they fill the pelt with enough gold that it would be covered up so not a hair could be seen.

loki went to rán, the goddess of the sea, and got a net, then returned to the pool and caught andvari in the form of a pike. he demanded as ransom all the dwarf's gold; when andvari had surrendered his entire hoard, loki noticed the dwarf held back one gold ring. andvari said with that ring he could reproduce the whole golden hoard; loki demanded the ring also. when andvari gave it to him, he pronounced this curse: "my treasure and this ring will be the death of all who own it."

loki brought the treasure to my father and covered up the otter-skin with all of it except the one ring. hreidmar saw that one hair was still exposed and demanded it be covered too. loki then put the last ring on it and the gods went their way. but soon thereafter my brother fáfnir killed my father for the treasure and took it to the top of gnita heath, making the gold his bed. he has become very evil, jealous that anyone should have any of the wealth but him, and has been transformed into a fierce dragon.

Sigurd and the birds
In this early 20th-century painting after a work by Ferdinand Lecke, Sigurd listens to the language of the birds. He gained the ability to understand the birds' language after drinking Fáfnir's blood.

"That is how I lost my inheritance," Regin concluded, "and this is how you can increase your wealth: deal the dragon his death and take the treasure." Sigurd said he would do it, but he needed a trusty sword in order to accomplish this feat; Regin said he would make him one sharp enough to slay Fáfnir, and the two made their agreement fast.

THE DEATH OF FÁFNIR

Regin made a sword and brought it to him; Sigurd struck the anvil with it and the blade broke. Regin made him another one and, just as before, it shattered on the anvil. Sigurd then went to his mother and asked her for the pieces of Gram, his father's sword. He took them to Regin's smithy. Regin heated them white-hot and struck with his hammer; sparks flew glittering in all directions, and with two blows he welded the pieces together, reforging the sword stronger than ever. Sigurd struck the anvil and easily cut it in two; then he plunged it edgewise into a stream and tossed in a tuft of wool a little up-current. When the wool drifted down against the sword's edge, it was cloven into two pieces and floated away, one on either side of the blade.

Sigurd took Gram into several battles and proved its worth, cleaving men, horses, heads, and helmets, returning home again with a great mass of wealth. At a banquet celebrating Sigurd's success, Regin whispered to him, "Now that you have venged your father and kinsmen, you should strike off Fáfnir's helmet and fulfill our agreement."

Sigurd slaying the dragon
IN THIS 19TH-CENTURY PAINTING AFTER A
WORK BY K. DIELITZ, THE HERO'S WEAPON
IS A SMALL KNIFE OR SHORT SWORD LIKE
BEOWULF'S; THE POINT OF INSERTION
BENEATH THE MONSTER'S LEFT SHOULDER IS
STEREOTYPICAL OF OLD NORSE SAGAS.

THE DRAGON'S BLOOD

Regin showed Sigurd the way to Gnita Heath, showed him Fáfnir's path, and told him to dig a trench across the path and get down in it. "When he crawls down to get water and crosses the trench," said Regin, "stab upward quickly with your sword and you will kill the dragon." Then he left.

Sigurd set himself to the task; but while he was digging, an old man with a long beard and a wide-brimmed hat appeared, saying it wasn't a very good idea to dig only one ditch.

The myth of Fáfnir

Hans Thoma's 1889 watercolor depicts the Continental version of the myth of Fáfnir and the Rhinegold popularized by Richard Wagner in *Siegfried* (1871); "Siegfried" is a variation of "Sigurd." Sigurds's stance appears almost operatic in implication.

"Dig one for the dragon's blood to flow into," he said, "but get in the other one and stab him from there." Then the old man vanished. Sigurd did as he was instructed.

Not long afterward, the dragon—huge, ferocious, spewing steam and poison in all directions around him—crawled down the path. He pulled his massive bulk into ponderous coils and stretched them out again, scraping the earth as he went. When the immense folds of the serpent's belly crossed the trench, the daylight was blotted out, and in total darkness Sigurd put the point to the dragon's flesh and shoved upward with all his might. The sword penetrated, and quickly Sigurd pushed until the entire blade, then the hilt, then his hand and arm went in all the way to his shoulder. He pulled Gram back out, covered with blood from his shoulder to the tip of the sword.

THE HOARD OF GOLD

When Fáfnir felt the wound, he began to writhe about, violently lashing his head and tail in his agonies. Sigurd leapt from his trench. The thrashing continued, then began to abate, until the dragon lay almost still. The monster's life was ebbing away; the trenches began to fill with the dragon's blood; faint tremors rippled here and there beneath the scaly flesh of the dying dragon.

Fáfnir's eyes grew dark, becoming blind with the approach of death. In his dying moments, his life fading away, Fáfnir struggled to look upon his killer. Then he spoke: "What is your name, and who urged you on to this deed?"

"My name is Sigurd, son of Sigmund; I was spurred by a keen mind, and my strong arm and sharp sword supported me in this venture."

"My hoard of gold will be your death," Fáfnir said.

"Everyone wants wealth from beginning to end," said Sigurd, "but an end to life is appointed to all, and each must die someday."

"You should ride from here quickly," said Fáfnir. "The mortally wounded often wreak revenge."

"Instead, I shall go to your barrow and claim your golden hoard," said Sigurd.

Fáfnir replied, "The gold you get on Gnita Heath will cost you your life—yours, and any who own it after." Then he was dead.

Sigurd slit the dragon open and carved out its heart. Regin appeared suddenly, drank his brother's blood, and told Sigurd to roast the heart and give it to him to eat. Sigurd built a fire, skewered the huge heart, and put it above the fire. As the heart cooked and blood oozed out in bubbling froth, Sigurd tasted it to see if it was done. When he put his finger to his lips, he instantly understood the language of birds in the branches nearby. "Here comes Regin," they said, "intent on murder, though Sigurd trusts him. Better kill than be killed!" they screeched. "Kill or be killed!" When Regin approached the fire, he called out gaily, "Hail Sigurd! Slayer of the dragon! How goes the cooking?" Sigurd drew Gram and struck off Regin's head. Then he ate Fáfnir's heart, went to his lair, loaded the treasure in his horse's saddle-bags, and rode off to other adventures.

FÁFNIR'S PROPHECY

In the years that followed, Fáfnir's dying prophecy came true. Sigurd had dragon images etched into his shield; his helmet, his saddle, and all the pieces of his armor were decorated with dragons so all would know he had slain the dragon.

Outfitted in this manner, Sigurd won the love of Brunhild. Under an enchantment, however, he married Gudrun, whose brothers Gunnar, Hogni, and Guttorm eventually killed Sigurd to gain his treasure. Each of these, in turn—including Niflung, Hogni's son—were slain in the violence provoked by the gold and the greed it incited around it. Sigurd, Brunhild, and their son Sigmund died in the plot surrounding Fáfnir's treasure.

Gudrun killed her second husband Atli and his two unnamed sons because of their bloodthirsty desire for the treasure. While Gudrun's third husband Jonakr was connected to Sigurd only through Gudrun, he and his sons Erp, Sorli, and Hamdir all were slain, as well as King Jormunrek and his son Randver, in the treachery spiraling around Gudrun and Svanhild, her daughter by Sigurd.

Portal relief of Sigurd
This detail from a 12th-century portal relief in Stave Church, in Hyllestad, Norway portrays Sigurd slaying the dragon with his sword, Nothung. Dragons were a prominent theme in Scandinavian wood carving in medieval times.

Sources: The adaptation of the Sigurd/Fáfnir myth is based directly on the original Old Norse material, combined with insights gleaned from modern English translations including the following: Jesse Byock, trans., *The Saga of the Völsungs: The Norse Epic of Sigurd the Dragon Slayer* (1990); Kevin Crossley-Holland, *The Norse Myths* (1980); Carolyne Larrington, trans., *The Poetic Edda* (1996); Lee M. Hollander, trans., *The Poetic Edda* (1962); Anthony Faulkes, trans., *Snorri Sturluson: Edda* (1987); Anthony Faulkes, trans., *Edda* (1987).

Sigurd fights the dragon

In the second Act of Wagner's *Siegfried*, the hero fights the dragon Fáfnir, who was once a human. Wagner based his story on the Old Norse myth in which Fáfnir's transformation into a dragon results both from his greed and from the curse pronounced upon the Rhinegold by the dwarf Andvari. This illustration was published in *Harper's Weekly* in 1887.

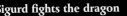

Thor and the Midgard Serpent

THE EARLY SCANDINAVIAN MYTHOLOGY PRESERVED IN *THE POETIC EDDA*, *THE PROSE EDDA*, AND *THE SAGA OF THE VÖLSUNGS* REVEALS A CONCEPTION OF THE DRAGON IDENTICAL TO THAT OF BEOWULF, IN WHICH THE MONSTER SYMBOLIZES THE DESTRUCTIVE POWER OF GREED. LIKE THOSE OF THE ANCIENT NEAR EAST, HOWEVER, THE ANCIENT MYTHS OF THE NORTH INCLUDE A COSMIC DRAGON WHOSE SYMBOLIC FUNCTION IS AMBIGUOUS. THE MIDGARDSORMR, OR IORMUNGANDR—THE "WORLD SERPENT"—OCCUPIES THE OUTER SEA SURROUNDING THE CIVILIZED WORLD, SEPARATING ORDER FROM CHAOS, BUT IT ALSO APPEARS ON DOOMSDAY AS A THREAT TO THAT SAME COSMIC ORDER. APOCALYPTIC ECHOES CANNOT BE IGNORED IN THIS RETELLING, NOR CAN WE SET ASIDE ECHOES OF THE ANCIENT MESOPOTAMIAN CREATION MYTHS, IN WHICH THE GODS STRUGGLE WITH MONSTERS OF THE SEA.

⋯⋯⋯⋯⋯⋯⋯⋯⋯⋯⋯⋯⋯⋯⋯⋯⋯⋯⋯⋯⋯⋯⋯⋯⋯⋯⋯⋯⋯

IN THE BEGINNING

The world began in fire and ice: two realms, the cold world of Niflheim and the hot lands of Muspilli. The ice began to melt, and the giant Ymir was born of the melt-waters. Ymir's cow now licked the ice, and slowly the form of a man was revealed: Buri, father of Bor, whose children were the gods Odin, Vili, and Ve.

Thor fishing for the serpent
THIS 18TH-CENTURY ICELANDIC DRAWING DEPICTS THOR FISHING FOR THE SERPENT OF MIDGARD FROM THE BOAT OF THE GIANT HYMIR.

Valhalla and the Midgard Serpent, 1680

The gods killed Ymir, and from his body they made the elements of the earth and heavens. Exploring the earth, they found two trees, whose trunks they made into a man and a woman. Midgard, the "middle enclosure" or "middle-earth," they fenced round with Ymir's eyelashes. Planted in the center of Midgard stood the World Tree, Yggdrasil, as a pillar, its roots going down into the well at the bottom of the underworld, its trunk anchoring the middle-world, the abode of men, and its branches upholding the roof of the heavens.

At the bottom, in the Well of Fate, at the roots of Yggdrasil, the dragon Nidhogg nibbled at the roots and gnawed the corpses of the dead. More snakes besides also lay there in the deep below: Góin and Móin—the sons of Grafvitnir—and Grábák and Grafvollud, Ofnir and Svafnir.

Jotunheim was the land of the giants, one of whom, the giantess Angrboda, bore three children by Loki: Fenriswolf, Iormungandr—the Midgard Serpent—and the goddess Hel. When the High God among the Aesir saw these three, he threw the serpent into the sea surrounding all the land. This serpent grew so large that it came to occupy the whole surrounding sea and bit its own tail. The High God threw Hel into Niflheim and made her custodian of the dead. Fenriswolf was taken to Asgard and reared by the war-god Tyr, the only one of the Aesir who dared draw near to it and feed it.

EIGHT CAULDRONS

On one occasion Thor bade Ægir, the Sea-god, brew beer for the high gods; Ægir grew angry and fought against Thor, defeating him; he then told Thor to get a cauldron from the giant Hymir in Élivág, the giants' land. Thor went there and arrived at nightfall accompanied by Tyr; when they arrived at Hymir's hall, they tried to hide, but when Hymir came home he saw them hiding behind a pillar, and at his first glance the beam above them broke asunder and fell upon them, disturbing the shelf upon which Hymir kept his eight cauldrons. All shattered but one. Fearful of these two gods who had often slain members of the giant clan, Hymir cooked three steers for their supper. But Thor was still hungry, and Hymir then offered to take him out in his boat to go fishing for more food.

THOR'S FISHING EXPEDITION

The next morning, Hymir rose early and Thor was up with him; he asked Hymir what to use for bait, and Hymir said, "get your own bait." So Thor found Hymir's herd, seized the largest ox of them all, and cut off its head. This he took to the shore where Hymir was preparing to launch his boat. He boarded the boat, and Hymir rowed them out into the middle of the sea. He stopped where he was accustomed to fish; but Thor wanted to go farther, even though Hymir warned that if they went too far out they would be in danger of encountering the Midgard Serpent.

They began to fish. Immediately Hymir caught two whales. But Thor did better: he put the ox-head on his hook and dangled it over the side, then lowered it to the ocean floor. The mighty Midgard Serpent stretched its jaws, engulfed the ox-head, and swallowed it whole. When it felt the hook, it jerked its head so hard that Thor's fists, holding tight to the line, were pulled down sharply against the side of the boat. It was caught; first it shrieked so loud the mountains shook; then it dived to the bottom. Thor strained at the line; the boat pitched and yawed, rose and fell upon the ocean, making huge waves in the struggle. Thor put his foot down so hard in the bottom of Hymir's boat that his foot went through until he was standing on the bottom of the ocean.

Thor pulled the monster up from the sea-bottom until it lay alongside the boat; Thor glared at the serpent and the serpent stared back at him, spewing poison. Finally Thor took his hammer Mjollnir and struck its head to kill it; he struck once but only stunned it, and the Midgard Serpent continued lashing furiously; Thor lifted his hammer a second time, but just as he raised it high, Hymir—frightened of the monster—took a knife and cut the line. As he did so, the monster gave one more furious heave, wriggled off the hook, and dived back down to the sea-bottom. Thor, enraged, threw his hammer after it. Some say with this blow he struck off the monster's head; but others report perhaps more correctly that the Midgard Serpent lies there still at the ocean's bottom in the encircling sea that surrounds all lands, where it will remain until Ragnarök, the Twilight of the Gods, at the end of the world.

TWILIGHT AND THE END

The Seeress spoke this prophecy:

" at the end, there will be three fierce winters in which frost and snow will blow upon mighty winds from all directions. the sun will shine, but without warming the earth, so there will be no summer between the three winters. fathers, sons, and brothers will kill each other without mercy because of their greed. it will be an age of axes, swords, and cloven shields, an age of wind, wolves, and the ruin of the world.

the earth will quake, mountains crumble, trees be uprooted, and all the bonds holding the earth will be broken. the mighty chain holding back fenriswolf will snap, and he will swallow sun, moon, and stars. the midgard serpent will swim ashore, setting forth floods that will engulf the land. flames spouting from its mouth and nostrils, fenriswolf will gape still wider, its snout against the roof of the sky and its lower jaw upon the ground. the midgard serpent will spew poison upon sea and sky; the skies will shine brighter than the sun as surtr comes forth with a shining sword.

there, on the battlefield named vigrid, heimdall will sound the mighty giallarhorn signaling the beginning of the end. yggdrasil will be shaken; the æsir will come forth in battle-gear: odin against fenriswolf and thor for a second encounter with midgardsormr. freyr will battle surtr and fall in the fight. garm, the hound of hell, will break loose and in its fight against tyr both will die. thor will have the victory over the midgardsormr, but once he has delivered its death-blow he will stagger back nine paces and then fall dead himself, overcome with the serpent's poison. this is the end of the world, the twilight of the gods. "

Sailors and sea monster

IN THIS UNDATED HAND-PAINTED ENGRAVING, SAILORS ATTEMPT TO SWIM ASHORE AFTER THEIR SHIP WAS CAPSIZED BY A SEA MONSTER.

Sailors on the back of a whale

Beowulf

THE STORY OF BEOWULF IS KNOWN FROM A SINGLE ANGLO-SAXON MANUSCRIPT DATING FROM THE LATE 10TH CENTURY. ALTHOUGH THE LANGUAGE OF THE POEM IS OLD ENGLISH, THE STORY IS SET ENTIRELY IN PREHISTORIC SCANDINAVIA—THE LEGENDARY RIVAL KINGDOMS OF THE DANES, THE SWEDES, AND THE GEATS— AMONG TRIBAL DYNASTIES ON THE NORTH-WESTERN COAST OF MODERN-DAY GERMANY AND FRISIA. THE POEM RECOUNTS THE MYTHIC FOUNDING OF DENMARK BY SCYLD/SKJÖLD, AND IN MENTIONING HENGEST, A JUTISH WAR-LEADER, IT EXHIBITS AFFINITIES WITH THE STORY OF THE 5TH-CENTURY FOUNDING OF ANGLO-SAXON ENGLAND BY A LEGENDARY FIGURE WITH THE SAME NAME. THE STORY OF BEOWULF'S FIGHT WITH A DRAGON, HOWEVER, PROBABLY ORIGINATED AS AN INDEPENDENT LEGEND IN A CYCLE OF NARRATIVES ASSOCIATED WITH THE MYTHICAL HERO.

THE GEATISH KINGDOM

The story begins many years after the young hero's return from a successful series of ventures fighting two troll-like monsters in Denmark. Shortly after his return to the Geatish kingdom, Beowulf's uncle, King Hygelac, was slain in battle against the Swedes; his young son Heardred assumed the throne but then was assassinated in a revenge killing perpetrated by Onela, king of an enemy tribe in Sweden. Beowulf assumed the throne and enjoyed fifty years of peaceful rule as king of the Geats until the disastrous attack of a fiery dragon.

Years later, after Hygelac and his son Heardred lay dead, rule of the Geats passed into Beowulf's hands. A good king, he ruled well for fifty years until—now old—his realm was threatened by a dragon. Its nightly rampages had wrought fiery destruction to the countryside surrounding King Beowulf's royal hall. Houses, farmsteads, fields, and whole villages had gone up in flames while the old king sat brooding on his throne. He had dealt with monsters before: as a boy, he had slain sea monsters, protecting his friend Breca during a swimming contest of five days in the open sea. He had delivered Hrothgar, King of Denmark, from the twelve-year-long scourge named Grendel, a man-eating troll of monstrous proportions; he had slain Grendel—ripping out his arm, and later decapitating him—and had killed the troll's mother in her underwater lair.

THE JEWELED GOBLET

But that was in his youth. Things were different now: the kingdom had lived in peace for fifty years; Beowulf had grown old, his people soft. He knew his warriors to be unaccustomed to fighting and ill-disposed to face an enemy—human or inhuman—and his kingdom was surrounded by rival kings he knew lusted after Geatish land, Geatish wealth, and his own throne. Now another problem had arisen, the worst of his long reign: a dragon, bent on destruction. Where had it come from? Why had it come?

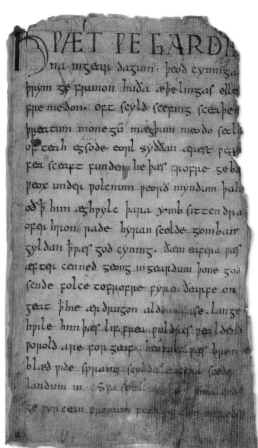

The 10th-century Anglo-Saxon manuscript of Beowulf, the oldest Germanic epic

THE OLD ENGLISH TEXT INCLUDES THE EARLIEST RECORDED REFERENCE TO THE DYNASTY OF SIGURD, GREATEST DRAGON-SLAYER OF NORTHERN MYTH. THE EPIC ENDS WHEN BEOWULF SIMILARLY SLAYS A GREAT MARAUDING DRAGON.

How could it be killed—indeed, who could kill it? These riddles went unsolved for many weeks, and the path of the dragon's destruction was growing longer and wider.

Alone in his royal hall—Geataburh, the seat of his power and his private residence—Beowulf sat pondering these things, the robes of his kingship loose around his frame. He sat gazing at his lap, absent-minded, fingering a jeweled goblet. The precious cup had been brought recently as a peace offering by a servant of his court, a nobody he had exiled for petty crimes—betrayal, lies, theft—an unimportant someone whose name he no longer knew. The day was drawing to its close; night approached.

The door at the far end of the empty hall opened quietly; a furtive figure slipped in and shuffled toward the throne. The thief had returned. He stood before Beowulf, his head hanging low, his hands clasped in supplication, hidden in his sleeves. He came with confessions, revelations, apologies. And answers to the riddles. All too late.

THE DRAGON'S CHAMBER

The thief told his story. Fleeing his king's presence, beaten and banished, he had made his way into the wastelands, the rocky coast of the raging sea, seeking refuge, a hiding place, repentant of his crimes but now an exiled wanderer. He had found a cave and gone in. Down a narrow passage, he had found a larger cavern. The sputtering light of his flickering torch cast shadows on the walls and ceiling of the underground chamber; but the flame also glittered in a thousand places on gems and ornaments, rich weapons and glittering armor—an enormous pile—

Beowulf shears off Grendel's head
(BACKGROUND IMAGE) THIS ILLUSTRATION DEPICTING BEOWULF IN THE ACT OF DECAPITATING THE MONSTROUS TROLL GRENDEL IS FROM HERO-MYTHS AND LEGENDS OF THE BRITISH RACE, 1918.

coins from far and wide, cups, platters, bejeweled shields, and all manner of priceless treasure heaped up, scattered on the floor of that ancient storehouse. And he had seen the cup—a golden chalice, gem-encrusted—with which he might buy back his lord's favor.

Little did he know, he said, of any danger; he knew nothing of the dragon brooding further in, in a deeper chamber. He had grabbed the cup and slipped out quickly—seen by no one—and made his way back to his lord. He had begged Beowulf's forgiveness, offered the cup as a token of peace, had laid it in his lap in a gesture of fealty, pledging his loyalty but refusing to say where the cup had come from.

THIEVERY AND RETRIBUTION

That was weeks ago. Beowulf had granted pardon but dismissed the man, returned him to his people but banished him forever from the king's presence. But the dragon's attacks had begun that very night. Now the thief had returned—breaking the ban—to tell the king the whole story. He had stolen the golden chalice from a dragon's hoard.

But what of the treasure? Where had it come from? Another riddle; only God knew the answer.

Death had taken them all, ancient owners of the dear treasures. The one who longest endured his tribe's diminishment lingered until only he was left, the last of his noble people. A lone survivor, he loaded up the treasure—patrimony of a people whose glory had faded—and bore it down to the headland to a hidden place, a cavern carved by the crashing sea, and there he placed it—immense treasure—before he died. The last survivor of a noble tribe, he entered the chamber and it became his tomb. His body rotted, his bone-house collapsed; but not long after, a dragon from parts unknown—borne aloft on serpent's wings—scented the treasure, entered the cavern, found the corpse, found also the gold piled in heaps, unguarded. He made it his lair, lay upon the hoard; three hundred years he had held it, hidden, unmolested, a marvel known to no one, as the lore-books say a dragon must do:

> " DRACA ON HLÆWE
> ᵹESECEAN SCEAL
> HORD ON HRUSAN,
> BEORHT ON BEARWE,
> ᵹRÆDIᵹ ON FRÆTWE,
> ON EORÐSCRÆFE NEARWE.
> ᵹRÆDIᵹ ON FRÆTWE. "

> " DRAᵹON SEEKS IN MOUND
> HOARD IN THE ᵹROUND,
> BRIᵹHT IN THE BARROW,
> ᵹREEDY IN TREASURE,
> IN EARTH CAVE NARROW. "

Study of a winged monster
This winged monster appears in a chalk and paper drawing by Michelangelo Buonarotti c. 1525.

Then the fugitive found the cave and filched the cup. Thus the dragon had begun its nightly raids upon the Geatish people, seeking revenge for the rape of his hoard.

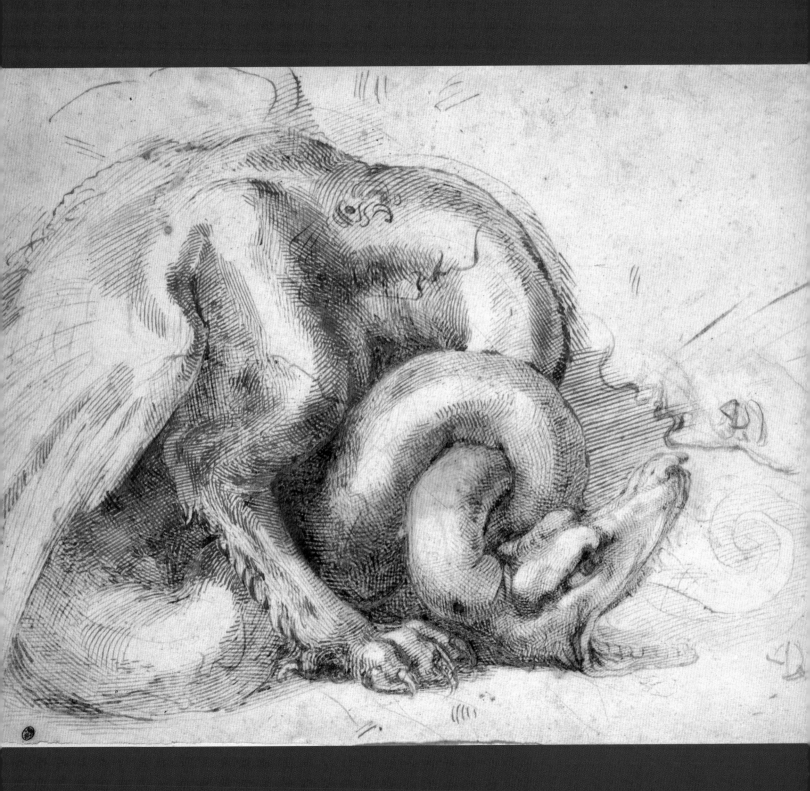

A TUMULT OF FLAME

Having finished his tale, the man who stole the cup stood before Beowulf abject, downcast, awaiting his fate. The shadows had lengthened; night had fallen. Beowulf sat silently, pondering anew his dire distress, turning over in his mind how to deal with his outcast servant. Suddenly there was a sound of rushing wind, the beating of great leathery wings; next there was a roar as if a blazing furnace, stoked to the flue, had been opened. In a shower of sparks and great waves of melting heat, the roof of Geataburh went up in flames. Roof beams fell blazing; pillars teetered, then fell, their tops already alight. Suddenly agile despite his years, Beowulf leapt from the throne, escaping the hall moments before the entire structure came toppling down in a tumult of flame. The fate of the thief—if he escaped with his life or perished in the hall—Beowulf never knew. In the night sky, the fiery dragon had already flown a long way off; he could just see its flame, tiny now on the west horizon as it circled over the sea and returned to its lair.

Dark thoughts seethed in Beowulf's heart, thoughts of revenge. The old lust for battle welled up again. But also the treasure weighed strong in his thoughts, preyed on his mind: in his long peaceful reign, he had ventured too little against foreign foes. Peacetime had brought too few spoils of war into his coffers; the tribe's treasury was almost exhausted; winning the dragon's hoard would change all that.

DEEDS OF GLORY

The next day Beowulf gathered a troop of ten of his most loyal men; he announced his intention to face the dragon himself in battle. The royal hall lay in ruins, a smouldering heap of smoking cinders. The men stood disheveled as Beowulf recounted the deeds of his youth, reminded them of his many victories, and vowed once more to enter the fray on behalf of his people.

"I will meet this monster," Beowulf boasted, "in a fight of requital, if the fiend dares come out of his cavernous lair. Deeds of glory such as you have not seen in all your lives I shall perform this day. Not one footstep will I take in retreat once the battle is joined. With glorious war I shall win the gold for the sake of my people. Either that," he concluded,

" OR DEATH WILL take me. "

With twelve men he embarked for the headland upon the cliff above the cavern where the dragon lay; eleven fled to the forest before they arrived. Only Wiglaf, Beowulf's kinsman, remained behind as a help to his leader.

With unnatural awareness, the sleeping dragon felt his foe's impending approach; the scaly worm, waiting encoiled, awoke on its hoard deep in its lair. Beowulf climbed down to the cave's mouth—an ancient stonework arch—and shouted his challenge to the monster within. A trail of steam issued in answer, then a smoky reek, then sheets of fire as the dragon flew from the cave. It shot high in the air in the broad light of day, circled wide, then descended like lightning and attacked the King of the Geats.

TRANSFORMATION: HUMAN TO DRAGON

Folklorists and mythographers including Jakob Grimm, Friedrich Panzer, G.V. Smithers, and Axel Olrik have found echoes of Beowulf's dragon widespread throughout Scandinavian oral tradition—many of which echo Fafnir's transformation from malevolent human to monstrous dragon in *the saga of the völsungs*.

✝

Beowulf and the dragon
HERE, THE OLD MAN BEOWULF
USES THE SHIELD OF HIS YOUNG
COMPANION WIGLAF TO DEFEND
HIMSELF AGAINST THE FIRE DRAGON.

THE GIANT-MADE SWORD

Their first encounter brought neither victory: the dragon's hide was proof against steely weapons; Beowulf carried an iron-bound shield specially made for the fiery meeting. The flames could not reach him; at Beowulf's first stroke, the sword glanced off, sparking against the scales of the dragon's flesh.

On the second attack, Wiglaf stepped forward to help his lord; the dragon spewed flames against the man, whose wooden shield could not withstand the fiery onslaught. Wiglaf took shelter beside his lord; the iron-wrought shield protected them both. Beowulf struck out again with his sword, hewed at the head of the fiendish dragon. The steel shattered on impenetrable scales; Nægling was splintered in useless shards: no mortal sword could match Beowulf's might.

The dragon came on for the third time now, attacked the king's neck, took him in its jaws, bit down hard with sharp fangs. Blood welled out in waves; Beowulf was wounded, swooned from the poison, the heat, the enormous pain. Heedless of the danger of the dragon's head, Wiglaf rushed to rescue his lord. He struck the monster in its mid-most parts, underneath, with a giant-made sword. It found entrance, went in, found its way home to the heart of the enemy. Instantly the fire began to abate, and Beowulf recovered his senses, renewed his attack with a battle blade aimed at the monster's belly. The knife cut; the dragon fell. The king and his thane had slain the serpent.

ASCENDING TO HEAVEN

But Beowulf was mortally wounded; Wiglaf laid him out on the ground not far from the dragon's smouldering corpse, removed his helmet, bathed his face, tended his lord. But the strong poison had already begun to work. Delirious, Beowulf began raving—demanded to gaze on the gold he had won by slaying the serpent. Obedient, Wiglaf entered the barrow, gathered an armload of precious objects, and carried them out where his lord lay dying. In his last moments, with his last breath, Beowulf gave thanks for the treasure—said it would serve to arm his troops, save his tribe, stave off conquest, buy victory. The old king gave up the ghost then, and his soul ascended, wound its way into the skies to seek the heaven of his fathers' gods.

A pyre was built on the headland above the dragon's den, in sight of the ruined hall, as a beacon for ships on the sea below. For long it stood as a memorial to the king who had vanquished all his foes, who—courageous to the last—gave up his life for the people he loved. He was a good king.

Beowulf's death

THE AGED KING BEOWULF DIES ACHIEVING THE GREATEST FEAT OF HIS HEROIC CAREER: SLAYING THE GEATISH DRAGON. HIS RESULTING TRAGIC DEATH BRINGS AN END TO HIS NOBLE DYNASTY AND SPELLS DOOM FOR THE TRIBE OF THE GEATS.

SOURCES: THIS TRANSLATION WAS MADE BY THE AUTHOR FROM THE ORIGINAL OLD ENGLISH TEXT: FRIEDRICH KLAEBER, ED., *BEOWULF AND THE FIGHT AT FINNSBURG*, 3RD ED. (1950). MANY EXCELLENT ENGLISH TRANSLATIONS EXIST, INCLUDING: ROY M. LIUZZA, *BEOWULF: A NEW VERSE TRANSLATION* (2000); SEAMUS HEANEY, *BEOWULF: A NEW VERSE TRANSLATION* (2000); MICHAEL ALEXANDER, *BEOWULF: A NEW VERSE TRANSLATION*, REV. ED. (2001); E.T. DONALDSON, *BEOWULF: A PROSE TRANSLATION* (2002).-

Medieval knights battle a dragon

WEAPONS OF ALL SORTS APPEAR IN MYTHS OF DRAGON-SLAYERS. IN ANCIENT NEAR EASTERN CREATION MYTHS, ARROWS ARE SHOT INTO THE BELLY OF THE PRIMORDIAL DRAGON OF THE WATERS. LATER MEDIEVAL STORIES FEATURE MAGIC SWORDS, KNIGHTS' SPEARS AND LANCES AND KNIVES. IN SACRED LEGENDS, HOLY WATER AND THE SIGN OF THE CROSS—OR SIMPLE PRAYER—ACHIEVE THE SAME PURPOSE.

Frotho, Fridlevus, and the Island Dragons

THE 13TH-CENTURY DANISH HISTORIAN, SAXO GRAMMATICUS— "SAXO THE GRAMMARIAN," OR PERHAPS, "SAXO THE LEARNED"— WROTE A LENGTHY LATIN HISTORY OF DENMARK CALLED THE *GESTA DANORUM*, "THE DEEDS OF THE DANES," COMPLETING IT SOMETIME BETWEEN 1208 AND 1223. THE FIRST NINE BOOKS CONCERN THE MYTHICAL PAST AND INCLUDE THE TWO STORIES BELOW. THERE ARE CLEAR PARALLELS BETWEEN THESE TWO EPISODES IN THE LIFE OF LEGENDARY DANISH RULERS, AND BETWEEN THEM AND OTHER DRAGON LEGENDS FROM THE EARLY MIDDLE AGES. JUST AS IN *BEOWULF* AND *THE SAGA OF THE VÖLSUNGS*, THE TWO HEROIC WARRIORS FIND, FIGHT, AND SLAY DRAGONS PRINCIPALLY BECAUSE THEY ARE THE POSSESSORS OF HOARDED TREASURES. THE DRAGON'S PROPENSITY TO GATHER AND POSSESS TREASURES IS EXPLORED PARTICULARLY, THOUGH NOT EXCLUSIVELY, IN THE GERMANIC WORLD.

FROTHO

King Hadingus was succeeded by his son Frotho, whose adventures were various and distinguished. When he was still but an adolescent, he displayed all the attributes of manhood. As a young king, Frotho did not allow himself to be corrupted by laziness or idle sport: he often withheld even the most common pleasures from himself and turned instead to the disciplines of military exercise, for he was forced by the circumstances of his reign to conduct armed campaigns in many parts of the northern world.

At length, the expense of these military operations became over-whelming, and the treasures which his father had amassed during his reign began to run out. Frotho no longer had the financial means with which to conduct any further campaigns, nor indeed even to maintain his army at home. For this reason, Frotho began to investigate the territories around him, searching desperately for any source of the supplies he needed for his country's defense.

SONG OF THE FARMER

One day, while engaged in this quest, he overheard the song of a rustic farmer; the music stirred him, and the words fired his imagination:

> Not far away an island lies, with lofty slopes.
> Its soft hills conceal a fortune;
> the island knows immense wealth.
> Deep within the mountain,
> a serpent entwined in spirals
> guards an enormous heap of gold;
> wound in circular coils,
> the dragon's sinewy tail lashes about
> while it spews voluminous gushes of poison.

Frotho spoke to the man and asked him where this dragon lay, and by what means he might succeed in claiming its hoard of treasure.

"If you wish to overcome that monster," said the farmer, "you must take the hide of a bull and stretch it over a shield. This shield you must take with you. But also you must cover your body with the skin of an ox: for if the serpent's acid venom comes into contact with your bare flesh, you would be consumed.

"Its three-pronged tongue flickers from its mouth, and its mouth spews horrific danger; but do not be dissuaded by its razor-sharp teeth, nor by the strength of its coils, nor by the venom it spews from its mouth. Keep your mind on courage, for although its scaly hide is impervious to the weapon of any man, know this: under the lowest part of its belly there is a weak spot. There an ordinary iron weapon can penetrate.

> " WITH THE POINT OF YOUR SWORD,
> FIND THIS SPOT! ONCE YOU HAVE FOUND IT,
> INSERT YOUR BLADE, PROBE THE SERPENT'S
> INSIDES. IN THIS WAY YOU WILL
> KILL THE DRAGON. "

THE DRAGON'S HOARD

The farmer gave further instructions to Frotho concerning the path to the mountain, where to dig down into the caves, and how to find the dragon's hoard. "Enter the caverns beneath the earth and carefully explore until you have found the treasure. Your bags will soon be filled with gold, and once you have regained your ship, you may sail it filled with treasure back to the shore of the mainland."

Frotho, believing all the farmer had said, did as he had been instructed. He prepared a shield covered with the hide of a bull, he covered himself in a garment made of ox-hide, and he sailed alone to the island. There he found the monster's path from the mountain to the water; there he lay in wait until the dragon returned toward its treasure-filled cave. Frotho leapt out and stabbed the dragon's flank with his sword. But the tough bristling hide turned the blow aside. The spears as well, which he threw at the dragon, sprang back without effect, defeating his efforts and preventing any injury to the monster, which was now becoming fierce with rage.

FEROCIOUS AGONY

When the dragon's thick hide had prevented him from killing it, Frotho remembered the farmer's words. Looking more closely, he could see the soft spot in its lower belly. He put the point of his sword to it and then shoved it in. Instantly the dragon began writhing in ferocious agony; but when it tried to bite him, Frotho raised his shield before him and its sharp teeth sank into the shield without touching him. Darting out its tongue in short rapid flicks, it spat out an enormous amount of poison, but then it breathed its last. Frotho made his way up the path to the mountain, dug down into the island's caverns, found the treasure, and sailed away with so much wealth in gold that he was now able to purchase a fleet of ships. So equipped, Frotho resumed his conquest of the lands around.

DRAGONS IN WATER

IN SCANDINAVIAN MYTHOLOGY, AS IN THE ANCIENT NEAR EAST, DRAGONS OFTEN LIVED IN OR NEAR THE WATER. MANY OLD NORSE SAGAS DESCRIBE HEROES' FIGHTS WITH DRAGON IN CAVES NEAR WATER OR ON PATHS LEADING TO A LAKE OR THE SEA; OFTEN, A FABULOUS TREASURE HIDDEN NEARBY IS THE HERO'S MOTIVE FOR SLAYING THE MONSTER.

✠

FRIDLEVUS

Once Amundi was slain, Fridlevus was finally freed from the threat of his fiercest enemy. Assured now of absolute peace, he gave up his former ferocious ways and turned to thoughts of love. He rebuilt his fleet, not for the purpose of war as before, but in order to pursue the pleasures of marriage which had been denied him earlier.

Fridlevus now set out upon a voyage of adventure. He sailed for a time into uncharted seas. But as luck would have it, the winds waned, failed, and died, and his fleet sat motionless in the still water. When his need for food became acute, he rowed from his ship in a small boat to shore. Pulling his skiff up onto the gritty beach, he journeyed inland, going through a wild landscape, until at least he stumbled into a village. There he met a man who called himself Grubbi. He was treated with great hospitality and fed and entertained for quite some time. At length, Fridlevus caught sight of Grubbi's daughter, and within a short time he fell in love with her. The two were married, fulfilling Fridlevus's fond desires. Soon she gave birth to a son, whom Fridlevus named Olaf.

THE DREAM

After a certain length of time, Fridlevus conquered Frogerth; and while making a difficult return voyage to his homeland, he was cast upon the shores of another uncharted island. Taking refuge in the woods uphill from the seaside, he fell asleep, weary from his journey. In his sleep, Fridlevus dreamt that he was encouraged by the strange apparition of an old man with a long beard, wearing a broad-brimmed hat, to unearth a treasure buried in the ground. He was told not only where the treasure was to be found but also how to avoid being overcome by the poison of the dragon that guarded it. The old man told Fridlevus to cover himself with the hide of an ox before approaching it, and to take a shield stretched with ox-hide as defense against the dragon's poisonous fangs. Fridlevus woke, did as instructed, and took his shield and his specially prepared garments down to the seaside to await the dragon's appearance.

SPOILS OF VICTORY

Fridlevus attacked the dragon as soon as it emerged from the waves. He shot his weapons against its scaly sides again and again, but without success: for the arrows were repelled by the dragon's crusted, scaly hide. The dragon thrashed about angrily with its exceedingly thick coils. With the powerful twisting of its coiled tail it grasped and uprooted the trees that got in its way. As it moved about, the thickness of the rest of its body made a trench steep on both sides, and soon the ground around it was hollowed out down to the bedrock. Finding the monster's upper portion to be invincible, Fridlevus then aimed at the lowest part of the belly with his sword; he pierced through the skin deep into its middle and then disemboweled its body even as it was writhing in its final agonizing moments. When at last it was dead, Fridlevus had the treasure dug up out of the ground and carried to his ships, making his way thence enriched with the dragon's fabulous wealth, which became the patrimony of his dynasty.

SOURCES: THIS TRANSLATION IS BASED UPON J. OLRIK AND H. RÆDER'S EDITION OF THE ORIGINAL LATIN, *SAXONIS GESTA DANORUM* (1931); HILDA ELLIS DAVIDSON AND PETER FISHER, TRANS., *SAXO GRAMMATICUS: THE HISTORY OF THE DANES* (2 VOLS., 2002); AND CHRISTINE RAUER, *BEOWULF AND THE DRAGON: SOURCES AND ANALOGUES* (2000).

The Red Dragon of Wales

Officially adopted as its national symbol in 1959, the Red Dragon has been associated with Welsh national identity since earliest history. In his 9th-century *History of Britain*, Nennius records that the red dragon symbolizes political independence of the British and eventual expulsion of the Saxon conquerors. In the previous centuries, Anglo-Saxon invaders had advanced relentlessly across the island, forcing native Britons to retreat westward to the portion of the island now defined by the national borders of Wales. But ironically, the mythic status of the red dragon as a Welsh national symbol may originate in battle-standards brought by the Britons' previous conquerors, the Romans, whose legions occupied the island during the first four centuries of the Christian era.

. . . .

UTHER PENDRAGON

Geoffrey of Monmouth's *History of the Kings of Britain* (c. 1136), on which the retelling below is based, elaborated significantly on the dragon myth. The epithet "Pendragon"—"head dragon" or "chief dragon"—applied to Uther at the end of this retelling has its own symbolic significance. Earlier in Geoffrey's *History*, when Uther sees a dragon-shaped comet in the night sky, Merlin interprets it as a portent of Uther's eventual success as a Welsh ruler.

KING VORTIGERN'S CASTLE

After the Saxons began to lay waste throughout the kingdom of the Britons, King Vortigern set out to build a castle upon Mount Snowdon. Each day, however, after the masons had laid the stones of the foundation, there was a disturbance deep in the earth that shook the foundation stones apart and destroyed the work they had done. After many days in which the same had happened, Vortigern called a council of wizards and entreated them to tell him by what means he might prevent the daily destruction of his fortification and thus stave off the conquest of his realm. The wizards told him to send throughout his kingdom to find a lad who was born without a father; Vortigern should slay the boy and sprinkle his blood upon the foundations which would then be so strong as to resist any siege.

Messengers went through all the kingdom without success. At last they came to a city called Carmarthen and watched as a group of young lads were playing at sport. In time an argument arose between two of the boys; one said; "Thou art a fool to have do with me, for I am born of kings on the mother and the father side. But who art thou, born to no man and no man's son!" The messengers learned the name of the second lad—Merlin.

Dragons as symbols of defense
FIGHTING RED AND WHITE DRAGONS—SYMBOLS OF WELSH DEFENSE AGAINST HOSTILE INVADERS—BENEATH VORTIGERN'S CASTLE. THE ILLUSTRATION IS FROM THE *VERSE CHRONICLE OF BRUTUS*, ORIGINALLY WRITTEN BY WACE IN THE 12TH CENTURY.

The Welsh flag

"Y Ddraig Goch ddyry cychwyn"—
"The red dragon will show the way."
Based in medieval heraldry, the "dragon
passant" appeared as the Welsh royal
badge in 1807. It displaced the image
of three white ostrich feathers as a
symbol of the Principality of Wales.
Queen Elizabeth II officially
recognized it in 1959.

The lad and his mother were summoned to Vortigern's court, and the lady told her story. When she was a damsel, there appeared in her chamber a handsome young man who held converse with her and kissed her, then vanished so she saw him no more. He returned to her many times, and on one occasion he lay with her and then vanished, leaving her great with child. The child was born and she called him Merlin Ambrosius. Then it was told to them how the wizards had said the lad's blood must be spilt upon the foundations of the tower, making it proof against any attack.

DRAGONS' CAVES

Hearing this, Merlin Ambrosius bade Vortigern summon the wizards, whereupon he would show how their report delivered to the King was a lie. He asked the wizards if they knew what lay beneath the foundations. The wizards declared that they knew not. Merlin commanded that workmen dig the soil beneath the foundation stones, and there they found a pool of water. "This pool maketh the soil above unstable," said Merlin, "and for this the foundations of the castle may not stand." Then he asked whether they knew what was beneath the pool; when the wizards declared they knew not, Merlin commanded the pool be drained, saying,

" O KING, WHEN THE POOL HATH BEEN REMOVED,
THOU SHALT FIND TWO CAVES BENEATH.
WHAT LIETH WITHIN THE CAVES IS
THE CAUSE OF ALL THY TROUBLE. "

So it was done, and all was found to be as Merlin had said. King Vortigern then went and sat beside the edge of the drained pool; as he watched, two dragons emerged from the caves, one white and the other red. As they approached each other, fire issued from their mouths and they then grappled with each other, each one striving for the mastery, until at length the white dragon overcame the red dragon and drove it to the edge of the pool that had been drained. But then the red dragon regathered its strength and overcame the white one. King Vortigern asked Merlin Ambrosius what this might signify.

MERLIN'S PROPHECY

Merlin said; "The Red Dragon betokeneth the race of the Britons and the White Dragon signifieth the Saxons whom thou has summoned hither to thy aid. But woe be unto the Red Dragon, for he shall be vanquished by the White Dragon, who shall occupy the caverns of the Red, in whose extermination shall all the mountains and valleys be made as a level plain. The streams shall overflow with blood. After long ages the Red Dragon shall return to his own and wreak vengeance upon himself; he that tills the soil shall till in vain, and many will leave their native soil and sow seed in plantations in foreign lands. Then the White Dragon shall arise and invite the daughter of the German Worm hither; so shall the gardens of Britain be planted with strange seed while the Red Dragon waits in torment at the far side of the pool. At last, after three hundred years, the German Worm shall find refuge no longer in the caverns of the White Dragon. The vengeance of our people shall be visited upon the White Dragon, its seed be uprooted from our garden, and its remnant be utterly decimated. All Wales will be filled with joy; Cornwall shall grow green once more; the foreigners shall be driven away and by the name of Brutus shall the island be called.

" IN THOSE DAYS SHALL LONDON BE ENCIRCLED BY A GREAT SERPENT THAT SHALL DEVOUR ALL THOSE THAT PASS BY; THE RAVEN AND THE KITE SHALL DEVOUR THE CORPSES OF THE SLAIN. A WORM WHOSE BREATH IS FIRE SHALL COME UPON THE LAND AND ITS VAPOR SHALL CONSUME THE TREES; THE STENCH OF ITS OFFSPRING SHALL CORRUPT WOMEN INTO HARLOTS. A GIANT SHALL ARISE AGAINST IT, BUT THE DRAGON OF WORCESTER SHALL RISE UP AGAINST THE GIANT; BUT IN THEIR STRUGGLE THE GIANT SHALL GAIN THE MASTERY. HE SHALL PUT OFF HIS GARMENTS AND MOUNT UPON THE BACK OF THE DRAGON NAKED, AND THE DRAGON SHALL CARRY HIM ALOFT, BEATING AT HIM WITH ITS TAIL. AT LAST THE GIANT WILL PIERCE THE DRAGON WITH HIS SWORD, AND THE DRAGON WILL DIE OF POISON, ENTANGLED IN THE COILS OF ITS OWN TAIL. "

**Battle of the red
and white dragons**

IN THIS 15TH-CENTURY MANUSCRIPT, A HOODED MERLIN EXPLAINS TO THE BRITISH KING VORTIGERN—ROBED IN ERMINE—THE SYMBOLIC SIGNIFICANCE OF THE FIGHTING DRAGONS.

King Vortigern marveled no less at the wit than at the predictions Merlin had made. Then Vortigern asked him by what death he should die, and Merlin foretold one of two: either the Saxons who sought to rule the land would overcome and slay him, or Aurelius and Uther Pendragon would seek to avenge their father's death upon him. Further, he foretold that on the morrow the Saxons would arrive with blood in their faces; Hengist would be slain and Aurelius Ambrosius would succeed as king. "He shall restore peace unto the land and restore the churches but die by poison. His brother likewise, succeeding him, shall die by poison also." On the next morning, Aurelius Ambrosius came into the land.

SOURCES: SEBASTIAN EVANS, TRANS., *HISTORY OF THE KINGS OF BRITAIN* (1963).

Red dragon

ENGRAVING OF THE OUROBOROS BY LUCAS
JENNIS FOR LAMPSPRINGCK'S *DE LAPIDE
PHILOSOPHICO, THE PHILOSOPHER'S STONE*
(1625). IMAGES OF DRAGONS BITING THEIR
TAILS EVOKE NEAR-EASTERN COSMOLOGY,
NORSE MYTHOLOGY'S WORLD-ENCIRCLING
MIDGARD SERPENT AND THE OUROBOROS
OF GREEK MYTH AND MEDIEVAL ALCHEMY.

Táin Bó Fráich

THE IRISH *TÁIN BÓ FRÁICH*, "THE CATTLE-RAID OF FRÁICH," SURVIVES IN FOUR 11TH-CENTURY MANUSCRIPTS, BUT THE OLD IRISH LANGUAGE OF THE STORY INDICATES THAT IT DATES FROM ABOUT THE 8TH CENTURY IN THE MYTHIC PREHISTORY OF IRISH CULTURE. THE STORY THAT COMES DOWN TO US IN THE MEDIEVAL MANUSCRIPT *THE YELLOW BOOK OF LECAN* FALLS INTO TWO PARTS. FIRST, THERE IS THE STORY OF FRÁICH'S WOOING OF FINDABAIR, CULMINATING IN FRÁICH'S SUCCESS IN KILLING A DRAGON AND ESCAPING ALIVE. IN THE SECOND PART, HE RETURNS HOME, FINDS HIS CATTLE HAVE BEEN STOLEN, AND EMBARKS ON AN ADVENTURE OVERSEAS TO RECOVER THEM.

. . . .

FRÁICH AND FINDABAIR

Raven-haired Fráich was the son of Idad of Connacht and Bofind of the Sídh. He was handsome, but he was not destined to live long. When he was a young man, his mother gave him twelve white cows. They had red ears: they were from the supernatural world of the Sídh. For seven years Fráich tended his cows alone; but in the eighth year of his bachelorhood, Findabair, the golden-haired daughter of Medb and Ailill, fell in love with him. All Ireland was inflamed with the gossip. At length, Fráich decided to go to Crúachan to see Findabair and ask her parents, Queen Medb, and King Ailill, for her hand.

First, however, Fráich went to the Sídh. There, he received lavish gifts from Bofind to take in wooing Findabair. The tally of these treasures is too long to tell, but among them were fifty mounted men in dark blue mantles, each with silver brooch-rings and pins of red gold; each had a white tunic embroidered in gold with the figures of animals. There were fifty silver shields with gold edges, fifty lances with bronze rivets, golden knobs, and spearheads embedded with carbuncle and adorned with precious gems. By night they shone as if illuminated by the midday sun. Bofind also gave him seven greyhounds with silver chains and bronze greaves, seven buglers with gold and silver horns, three harpists and three jesters wearing silver and golden crowns, and other extraordinary gifts too numerous to mention.

A SPLENDID COMPANY

The watchman who saw their coming to the royal dún at Crúachan said he had never seen a more splendid host in finer array than these. Fráich's company arrived at the doors; they set their hounds free to chase seven deer, seven foxes, seven hares, seven wild boars, and seven otters. All were slaughtered before the dún and offered to their hosts.

The company were welcomed, and a quarter of the house was apportioned to Fráich and his men. It was a splendid house constructed of red yew and pine, and decorated sumptuously with copper pillars, copper facings on the door panels, and many silver and gold adornments throughout. While harpists played on marvelous instruments, Medb and Fráich began a game of fidchell. The music was so exquisitely played and so excruciatingly beautiful that twelve men died hearing it.

FRÁICH AND
BEOWULF

JAMES F. CAMPBELL'S
"THE CELTIC DRAGON
MYTH" (1911), IN WHICH
THE SON OF A POOR
FISHERMAN FIGHTS A
THREE-HEADED DRAGON,
IS COMPILED FROM
A DOZEN HIGHLAND
SCOTS FOLKTALES. SOME
HAVE SUGGESTED A
CONNECTION BETWEEN
THE BEOWULF STORY AND
CELTIC TRADITION—
WHETHER OR NOT THIS
IS THE CASE PROBABLY
CANNOT BE ANSWERED.
WE CAN BE SURE,
HOWEVER, THAT THE
CELTIC WORLD HAD A
MYTHIC TRADITION THAT
INCLUDED DRAGONS
OF THE SORT
REVEALED HERE.

✠

The fidchell game lasted a long time, lit by the glowing jewels of Fráich's men's arms. At length Medb said, "This is the longest day I have ever spent in this dún." Fráich answered, "So it would be: we have played now for three days and three nights; I have not beaten you in the game for fear of dishonoring you." Then Medb rose, ashamed: deceived by the light of Fráich's jewels and distracted by the game, she had not given their guests any food in all that time. The guests were fed, and they stayed there for three more days and nights. When Ailill invited them to stay as long as they liked, Fráich replied, "We will remain for another week or so." They stayed for two weeks, hunting each day near to the dún.

THE BRIDE-PRICE

In all this time, Fráich had not spoken to Findabair, though it was to visit her that he had come to begin with. At dawn one morning he rose to bathe in the loch. So also did Findabair. When they met at the water's edge, Fráich took her by the hand and asked her to come away with him. "That I will not do freely," she said. "Though I am the king's daughter, you are not so poor that you cannot easily win me in the proper manner. Then perhaps I might choose to go with you." She gave him as a token a thumb-ring given to her by her father. They parted.

The gossip concerning Findabair's love for Fráich and Fráich's affection for Findabair had not escaped the attention of Medb and Ailill, who became concerned that the two might run away together. However, Medb said it would be to their own advantage for them to do so, if Fráich could be persuaded to return with his twelve supernatural cows and assist them in raiding the herd of Cúailnge. Just then, Fráich entered the chamber and asked to speak to the king and queen. They agreed, and he immediately asked, "Will you give me your daughter?"

"So we will," said Ailill, "provided you pay the bride-price."

"And what price would that be?" asked Fráich.

Ailill answered: sixty grey horses with gold bits and bridles; twelve cows, each with a white calf with red ears. "They must come with your whole company and all your musicians," Ailill said, "and you must help us raid the cattle from Cúailnge." Incensed, Fráich refused, saying he would not pay that much even for the hand of Medb herself; he rose immediately and left their chamber.

Ailill and Medb agreed that if Fráich took Findabair unpaid for, the other kings of Ireland would besiege them in their apparent weakness; it would be better to kill Fráich there and then, even at the risk of dishonor. Ailill said he would see to it that no dishonor would come to them.

ROWAN BERRIES

On an island near the southern shore of Loch Medb there grew a rowan tree that bore sweet red berries. One taste of its fruit was said to end the pangs of hunger, and its juice was believed to cure mortal diseases. Ailill sent a message to Fráich saying Queen Medb had fallen ill. Fráich was told to go to the island and gather a handful of rowan berries to cure her. But both he and Medb knew this rowan tree was guarded by a dragon.

FRÁICH

THE EARLIER LEGEND ASCRIBES TO FRÁICH A DRAGON-FIGHT SIMILAR TO BEOWULF'S. IN A LATER VERSION, FRÁICH SURVIVES HIS ENCOUNTER WITH THE DRAGON OF LOCH MEDB AND CONDUCTS A RAID TO RECOVER HIS STOLEN HERDS. THE TÁIN BÓ FRÁICH WAS INFLUENCED BY THE TÁIN BÓ CUAILNGE, "THE CATTLE-RAID OF COOLEY," ONE OF THE OLDEST VERNACULAR NARRATIVES IN ANY EUROPEAN LANGUAGE.

✦

Fráich and Ailill went to the shore of the loch. Fráich looked at the dark water and asked, "What sort of lake is this?" Ailill answered, "There is no danger here so far as we know, and we are accustomed to bathe here frequently. Besides," he said, "you are reputed to be an excellent swimmer." Fráich stripped, leaving his clothing on the bank, and entered the water. He swam across to the island. There he found the rowan tree just as had been told to him. There also he saw a fierce dragon curled around the tree. Its mouth was open, and it was asleep.

Fráich stole past the monster, plucked a handful of berries, and swam back across the loch undetected. He took the berries to Queen Medb. But when he gave them to her, she said she needed now a branch from the tree in order to be made completely well.

BLACK WATER

Fráich went to Loch Medb again, though this time he was followed secretly by Findabair, carrying a sword. Unbeknown to Findabair, her father Ailill also followed in secret. Fráich stripped and swam across to the island a second time. He stole past the dragon, seized the tree by its top branches, and pulled it up by the roots. Then he went into the water and swam toward the shore with the rowan branch across his shoulders. Forever afterward, Findabair said that she had never seen anything more beautiful than the cluster of red berries against Fráich's white body in the dark water, his narrow, handsome face, and his blue eyes shining beneath his black locks.

This time, however, the dragon woke and was aware of him. When Fráich was halfway across, the monster entered the loch and swam toward him. Just as Fráich reached the shore, the dragon took him in its jaws. In hiding, Findabair watched as the dragon tore Fráich's arm off. The boulders on the shoreline were stained red with the blood that flowed from the mortal wound.

Findabair took off her clothing and dived into the water with the sword she had brought. Despite his wounds, Fráich saw that the naked, golden-haired Findabair was the most beautiful woman he had ever seen. Just at that moment, Ailill stepped out of hiding and threw a five-pointed spear at Fráich, intending to kill him. But Fráich caught it in his remaining hand and threw it back at Ailill, just missing him but piercing his outer cloak and inner tunic. Findabair put the sword into Fráich's hand and swam away. Fráich swung the sword, cut off the dragon's head, and swam back to shore. He threw the head and corpse of the dragon onto the scree, and dragged himself onto the shore. He was alive, but he was mortally wounded. Findabair fainted in fear.

When she awoke, she found her hand nestled in Fráich's bloodstained hand. "Now you have become food for birds of prey," she said, "but for this deed forever will you be renowned in the world." Then Fráich died. The loch forever bears the name Loch Medb, and the place where, dying, Fráich killed the dragon, is called Dublind Fráich—"Fráich's Black-water."

SOURCES: J.F. CAMPBELL, *THE CELTIC DRAGON MYTH* (1911; RPT. 1981).

Further Reading

The bibliography on dragons, dragon-slayers, dragon myths, and dragon-lore is enormous. Dragon myths have been documented and interpreted by mythographers, religious historians, and literary scholars. They also have attracted the attention of non-specialists, and the intellectual value of their investigations—while admirably enthusiastic—is undercut by the relative lack of scholarly credentials necessary to guarantee reliable results. In addition to the sources cited at the end of each chapter, readers who wish to pursue the subject further may consult the following works profitably.

Armour, Robert. *Gods and Myths of Ancient Egypt.* Cairo: American University in Cairo Press, 2001.

Bates, Roy. *Chinese Dragons.* New York: Oxford, 2002.

Birrell, Anne. *Chinese Myths.* Austin, TX: University of Texas Press, 2000.

Blanpied, P. W. *Dragons.* New York: Random House, 1980.

Brown, Norman O. *Hesiod: Theogony.* London: Macmillan, 1985.

Budge, E. A. Wallis. *The Gods of the Egyptians.* London: Kegan Paul, 2005.

Child, C. G. "The Natural History of the Dragon," in *University of Pennsylvania Lectures,* vol. 7 (1921): 103–124; Odell Shepard and Arthur Adams, eds. *In Honor of the Ninetieth Birthday of Charles Frederick Johnson, Professor of English in Trinity College, 1883–1906. Papers, Essays, and Stories by his Former Students.* Hartford, Ct.: Trinity College, 1928. 101–130.

Clark, R. T. Rundle. *Myth and Symbol in Ancient Egypt.* London: Thames and Hudson, 1991.

Coogan, Michael David. *Stories from Ancient Canaan.* Philadelphia: Westminster Press, 1978.

Crossley-Holland, Kevin. *The Norse Myths.* New York: Pantheon, 1980.

Dalley, Stephanie. *Myths from Mesopotamia.* New York and Oxford: Oxford University Press, 1989.

Davis, F. Hadland. *Myths and Legends of Japan.* New York: Dover, 1992.

Day, John. *God's Conflict With the Dragon and the Sea: Echoes of a Canaanite Myth in the Old Testament.* Cambridge: Cambridge University Press, 1985.

De Visser, M. W. *The Dragon in China and Japan.* Amsterdam: J. Müller, 1913.

Dickinson, Peter. *The Flight of Dragons.* New York: Harper & Row, 1979.

Ellis-Davidson, Hilda R. *Gods and Myths of the Viking Age.* New York: Bell, 1981.

Evans, Jonathan D. *"Dragon" In Medieval Folklore: An Encyclopedia of Myths, Legends, Tales, Beliefs, and Customs,* eds. Carl Lindahl, John McNamara, and John Lindow. Santa Barbara, CA: ABC-CLIO, 2000. 233–240.

Evans, Jonathan D. *"The Dragon" In Mythical and Fabulous Beasts: A Sourcebook and Research Guide,* ed. Malcolm South. Westport, CT.: Greenwood, 1987. 27–58.

Evans, Jonathan D. "As Rare as They are Dire: Old Norse Dragons, Beowulf, and the Deutsche Mythologie". In *The Shadow-Walkers: Jacob Grimm's Mythology of the Monstrous,* ed. Tom Shippey. Turnhout: Brepols, 2005. 217–69.

Evelyn-White, H. G. trans. *Hesiod, Homeric Hymns, Epic Cycle, Homerica.* Cambridge: Harvard University Press, 1914.

Fontenrose, Joseph. *Python: A study of Delphic Myth and its Origins.* Berkeley, CA: University of California Press, 1959.

Frazer, James G., ed. and trans. *Apollodorus: The Library.* Cambridge: Harvard University Press, 1921.

Gantz, Timothy. *Early Greek Myth: A Guide to Literary and Artistic Sources.* Baltimore, MD: Johns Hopkins, 1993.

Griffith, Ralph. *The Hymns of the Rig Veda.* Varanasi: Chowkhamba Sanskrit Series Office, 1963.

Hathorn, Richmond Y. *Greek Mythology.* Syracuse: Syracuse University Press, 1977.

Hayes, L. Newton. *The Chinese Dragon.* 3rd ed. Shanghai: Commercial Press, 1923.

Heidel, Alexander. *The Babylonian Genesis.* Chicago, IL: University of Chicago Press, 1951.

Henken, Elissa R. *Traditions of the Welsh Saints.* Cambridge: D. S. Brewer, 1987.

Hogarth, Peter, and Val Clery. *Dragons.* New York: Viking, 1979.

Ingersoll, Ernest. *Dragons and Dragon Lore.* New York: Payson & Clarke, 1928.

Jensen, S. R. *Beowulf and the Battle-Beasts of Yore.* Sydney: ARRC, 1994.

Jensen, S. R. *Beowulf and the Swedish Dragon.* Sydney: ARRC, 1993.

Johnsgard, Paul A., and Karin Johnsgard. *Dragons and Unicorns: A Natural History.* New York: St. Martin's, 1982.

Jones, David E. *An Instinct for Dragons.* New York: Routledge, 2000.

Kapelrud, Arvid S. *Baal in the Ras Shamra Texts.* Copenhagen: G. E. C. Gad, 1952.

Kloos, Carola. *Yhwh's Combat with the Sea: A Canaanite Tradition in the Religion of Ancient Israel.* Leiden: E. J. Brill, 1986.

Lionarons, Joyce. *The Medieval Dragon: The Nature of the Beast in Germanic Literature.* Middlesex: Hisarlik Press, 1998.

Macdonnell, A. A. *The Vedic Mythology.* Delhi: Indological Book House, 1971.

Maurer, Walter H., trans. *Pinnacles of India's Past.* Amsterdam: John Benjamins, 1986.

McCall, Henrietta. *Mesopotamian Myths.* London: British Museum Press, 1990.

Morgan, Harry T. *Chinese Symbols and Superstitions.* Perkins: South Pasadena, CA, 1942.

Nilsson, M. P. *The Mycenaean Origins of Greek Mythology.* 1932; repr. Berkeley, CA: University of California Press, 1972.

O'Brien, Julia M. and Fred L. Horton, Jr. *The Yahweh/Baal Confrontation and Other Studies in Biblical Literature and Archaeology.* Lewiston, New York: Edwin Mellen, 1995.

O'Flaherty, Wendy., trans. *The Rig Veda.* New York: Penguin, 1981.

Parker, Simon B., ed. *Ugaritic Narrative Poetry.* Atlanta, GA: Scholars Press, 1997.

Piggott, Juliet. *Japanese Mythology.* New York: Peter Bedrick Books, 1983.

Rauer, Christine. *Beowulf and the Dragon.* London: D. S. Brewer, 2000.

Rose, H .J., *A Handbook of Greek Mythology.* 1928; repr. London & New York: Routledge, 1991.

Ruppert, Donna. *Dragon's Path.* San Rafael, CA: DawneLeigh, 1979.

Smith, Mark S. *The Ugaritic Baal Cycle.* Leiden: E. J. Brill, 1994.

Strassberg, Richard E. *Chinese Bestiary: Strange Creatures from the Guideways Through Mountains and Seas.* Berkeley, CA: University of California Press, 2002.

Thomas, Winton D., ed. *Documents from Old Testament Times.* New York: Harper & Row, 1958.

Tripp, Raymond P. *More About the Fight With the Dragon.* Lanham, MD: University Press of America, 1983.

Visser, M. W., ed. *The Dragon in China and Japan.* Amsterdam: Müller, 1913.

Walls, Jan and Yvonne Walls., ed. and trans. *Classical Chinese Myths.* Hong Kong: Joint Publishing Company, 1984.

Watkins, Calvert. *How to Kill a Dragon.* New York and Oxford: Oxford University Press, 1995.

Werner, E. T. C. *Ancient Tales and Folklore of China.* London: Bracken, 1986.

Whyman, Alison, and Wendy Bramall. *Discovering Dragons.* London: British Museum, 1986.

Wyatt, N. *Religious Texts from Ugarit.* London & New York: Sheffield, 2002.

Yang, Lihui. *Handbook of Chinese Mythology.* Santa Barbara, CA.: ABC-CLIO, 2005.

Yuan Ke. *Dragons and Dynasties: An Introduction to Chinese Mythology.* London & New York: Penguin, 1993.

Zhao, Quiguang. *A Study of Dragons, East and West.* New York: Peter Lang, 1992.

Index

A

Acheloos 98–9

Acrisius 108, 113

Aditi 37–8

Aeetes 91, 92

Aegir 147

Aesir 146, 149

Aeson 89

Agatamori 27

Agenor 86

Ailill 178, 180–2, 183

Alkeides 97–8

Alkmene 96–7

Ambrosius Merlin 172–4

Ammon 126–7

Amphitryon 96–7

Anat 53, 54

Andromeda 108–15

Andvari 135

Anshar 62

Anthony, St. Gatefold 2

Apep 21, 40, 43–5

Apollo 80–5

Apsu 59, 60–1, 65

Ares 87

Asherah 50, 53, 55

Athena 77, 82, 89, 91, 92, 111

Aurelius Ambrosius 174

B

Baal 20, 49, 50–7, 58

Bates, Roy Gatefold 1, 9

Bel 58

Beowulf 15, 74, 152–61

Bevis of Hampton 118

boat festival Gatefold 1

bones Gatefold 1

Brunhild 140

C

Cadmus 86–9, 91

Cephus 111, 112

Ch'ih Yu 22

Child, C.G. 8

Chiron 89–90

Ch'u Yuan Gatefold 1

Cilix 86

clouds Gatefold 1

Colchis 90–1

D

Damkina 61

Danae 108, 112–13

deafness Gatefold 1

Deïaneira 98–9

Delphyne 77, 78, 80

Dictys 110, 112–13

Dol 126, 128

Dragon Gate 29

Dragon Kings Gatefold 1, 14, 26–35

E

Ea 60–1, 62–3

Echidna 100

El 49, 50–3, 54, 55

Elektryon 96

Enuma Elish 58, 67

Epimethus 81–2

Euripedes 80

Europa 86

Eurystheus 96, 97, 98, 99, 102

Eurytion 101

eyesight Gatefold 1

F

Fáfnir 74, 130–43

Fenriswolf 146, 149

Findabair 178–9, 180, 182–3

Fontenrose, Joseph 8, 22, 23, 71,
    72

Fráich 178–83

Frankfort, Henri 72

Freyr 149

Fridlevus 168–9

Frotho 164–7

G

Geoffrey of Monmouth 170–1

George, St. 15, 107, 108, 116–25

Geryon 101

Glauce 95

Goff, Jacques le 74

Golden Fleece 90, 91, 92

Gorgons 108, 110–11

Grendel 153

Grubbi 168

Gudrun 140

H

Hadingus, King 164

Harmonia 86

Heardred 152–3

Hel 146

Hengest 152

Hephaestus 78

Hera 77, 80, 97, 98, 102

Herakles (Hercules)
    77, 90, 96–103

Hermes 78, 111

Hikohohodemi 28

Hjalprek 133

Hjordis 132–3

Horus 44–5

Hreidmar 135

Hrothgar 153

Hydra 100–1

Hygelac, King 152

Hymir 147–8

I

I-Ching 21

Indra 8, 20, 36–9

Iphikles 97

Izanagi 26

J

Jason 86, 89–95

John, St. 104, 106

K

Kingu 62, 65

Kothar-u-Kasis
    54–5, 56

Kreon, King 98

L

Labbu 58

Ladon 102–3

Leto 80, 84

Li Hsia Gatefold 1

Loki 135, 146

Lyngvi 132

M

Marduk 8, 20, 58–67

Margaret of Antioch, St.
   Gatefold 2

Martha of Bethany, St.
   Gatefold 2

Medb 178, 179–82

Medea 91, 92–5

Medusa 110–11, 112

Megara 98

Menippe 97

Merlin 171, 172–4

Michael, St. Gatefold 2, 104–7

Midgard Serpent 15, 144–51

Mot 49, 55

Mummu 59, 60

N

Nagas Gatefold 1, 8

Neleus 89

Nennius 170

Nereus 103

Nidhogg 146

Nihongi 26

Ninurta 58

O

Odin 131, 135, 149

Ohowatatsumi 26, 28

Olybrius Gatefold 2

Onela 153

Otohime 30–1, 34–5

Otr 135

P

Pelias 89, 90, 94

Pental 128–9

Perseus 108–15

Phineas 112

Phoenix 86

Polydectes 110,
   112–13

Poseidon 82, 89, 103,
   110, 111, 112

Prometheus 82

Python 77, 80–5

R

Ra 21, 40–5

Red dragon 170–5

Regin 133–7, 139

Rig Veda 20, 37

river dragons Gatefold 1

S

Samson, St 126–9

Satan Gatefold 2

Saxo Grammaticus 164

sea dragons Gatefold 1,
   26–35, 49–57

Set 21, 40, 45

Shan Hai Jing Gatefold 1

Shèn Yi 22

Shu Ching 22

Siggeir 132

Sigmund 131–2

Sigurd 15, 74, 130–43

Silvester, St. Gatefold 2

Spartoi 89

Spenser, Edmund 75

T

Táin Bó Fráich 178–83

Tarasconus Gatefold 2

Thespios 98

Thor 15, 144–51

Ti'amat 8, 20, 58–66

Tolkien, J.R.R. 16, 75

Toyotamabime 28

Triton 103

The True Dragon Gatefold 1

Typhon 76–9, 100

U

Ugarit 49

Urashima 28, 30–5

ur-myth 71

Uther 170–1, 174

V

Voragine, Jacobus de 118

Vortigern, King 171–4

Vritra 8, 20, 36, 38–9

W

Wang Fu Gatefold 1

Watkins, Calvert 71

Welsh dragon 170–5

Wiglaf 159, 160–1

Williams, Jay 16

Y

Yahweh Gatefold 2,
    20, 49, 58

Yamm 20, 49, 50–7

Yellow Emperor Gatefold 1

Yggdrasil 146, 149

Yi 22

Ying Lung 22

Ymir 144, 146

Yü 22

Z

Zaphon, Mount 50, 54–5

Zeus 76–9, 80, 82,
    84, 86, 97, 108, 110

Zu 58

ACKNOWLEDGMENTS

Dr. Verlyn Flieger of the University of Maryland is hereby gratefully acknowledged for her crucial role in bringing together the author and the publishers for the project that resulted in this book. Additionally, I acknowledge my indebtedness to my colleague at the University of Georgia, Dr. Elissa R. Henken, whose work on Welsh hagiography was informative at an important stage for the chapter on St. Samson. Dr. Ted Lewis, the Blum-Iwry Professor of Near-Eastern Studies at Johns Hopkins University, gave advice long ago on sources, and his own pathbreaking work on Ancient Near-Eastern myths made composition of the relevant chapters here much easier. I recognize the long-term benefits afforded by discussions over the years with Dr. Joyce Lionarons of Ursinus College and Dr. Christine Rauer of the University of St. Andrews concerning the subjects treated in the chapters on Beowulf and the Old Norse myths. The late Dr. Raymond P. Tripp, Professor Emeritus at the University of Denver, also proved to be an enthusiastic—if often entertainingly idiosyncratic—interlocutor concerning just what really is happening in the last part of Beowulf, until he passed away in 2005. My colleagues at the University of Georgia, Dr. Simon Gatrell and Dr. James Nagel, gave sound advice on the particulars of this publication project, for which I am appreciative. Most of all, I am deeply grateful to my family—Susan, and John David, Anna, and Owen—who deserve special thanks for weathering the hardships of the intensive period of research and writing necessary to meet deadlines and complete the book.

PICTURE CREDITS